G000272447

Publisher

© MYSTIS & CO.
108 Menelaou Parlama st.
71 500 Heraklion Crete
Tel. 2810 346451,   fax : 2810 221908
www.mystis.gr / info@mystis.gr

Author

Antonis Alibertis, Naturalist
12 Atalantis st. Heraklion, Crete / +302810323398

Publisher Design   Galanis Th. Ioannis
Cover   Galanis Th. Ioannis

Photography   Antonis Alibertis

Translation-Redaction Zoe Antonopoulou

Print

TYPOCRETA
Industrial Area of Heraklion, Crete
+302810380882-6
www.kazanakis.gr
info@kazanakis.gr

1

PREFACE

Dear reader, in this book we will not spread ourselves on the relief of Crete nor its formation through the millions of years since the island appearance on the world map. We will not illustrate in detail its climate or the microclimates that dominate the mountains or gorges. Nor will we research the variform reserves and water-reserves. Our aim in this small book is to help the visitor, either Greek or non-Greek, to be able to identify, relatively easy, the more than 270 wild flowers, picked out among so many (there are more than 1500 species) on this book, which are blossoming during the year and admire them at ease.

This book is divided into four parts, according to the seasons. Each part classifies the flowers which blossom at that particular season. It is obvious, though, that some of the flowers appear just before, or after the season, in which they are classified. You see, flowering does not stop because there is a change of season. For example, we all know that during winter, an extended fair weather will urge many plants to blossom earlier. Similarly, a heavy winter will delay the flowering. In Crete, this phenomenon is even more profound. There are plants which will blossom on a non-expecting season and still others which will extend their flowering for much longer periods of time.

The 270 classified plants of this book are not necessarily the commonest, or the most unexceptional; on the contrary, some of them are considered to be rare and hard to find. In this way we would like to show that the Flora of Crete is not as easy to uncover, as we would like it to be. Indeed, some of the Cretan native plants which are more than 180, are connected to biotopes so confined and microclimates so unique, that are seen only at some specific areas, like the proud mountains or the deep gorges of the isle. More than that, the specific location of the island, which is between the Libyan and the Aegean Sea, on the crossroad of three continents – Europe, Asia and Africa – has deeply affected its Flora.

Consequently, most of the plants of Crete originate from Europe, second come the plants from Asia, while the ones, which migrated from Africa, are few and onfined to the southern areas of the island and on the small islands, south of Crete on the Libyan Sea. In this book, the European origin of flowers is not mentioned, however, if the origin is Asian or African it will be mentioned, so that you can form a better picture of the data.

We also mention the fluctuating size of the plant, its main characteristics, the altitude, in which it is seen, its basic qualities (poisonous, pharmaceutical, edible, ornamental, aromatic) and, as objective as can be, its prevalence on the island.

For your own convenience:

The time of the seasons follow the scientific criteria: Spring starts on 21st March, summer on 21st June, autumn on 23rd Sept and winter on 21st December.

2. The months of the flowering follow the Latin numerical system I, II, III, IV, V and so on.
A dot (●) in front of the Latin name of the plant is an indication of the native plants of Crete.

Synonyms are given when necessary.

5. Also mentioned is the family of the plant.

The common names and the translation of the scientific Latin names are given, whenever possible.

7. The plant's size is determined, using a specific design.

8. The prevalence and consistency of the plant's appearance is determined with black dots on the map of Crete. The more the dots, the commonest the plant.

9. The vegetation zones (1.by the sea, 2.lowland, 3.montain, 4.subalpine and alpine) are determined, as their combination, using specific designs.

10. The immediate, apparent information is given using certain symbolisms, relative to the class of the plant.

5 **Aristolochiaceae:**

3

● *Aristolochia cretica* **Lam.**

Cretan Birthwort
6

8 **9** **7** 60cm 30cm **10** **2** **III-IV**

INDEX

Ranunculus asiaticus & orchis italica

Apiaceae:

Daucus carota L.

III-VII

Biennial aromatic plant. Nodular rhizome, robust and hairy stem, leaves lanceolate and umbels large, with many white flowers, mid-flower often dark purple. Following flowering, the umbel bends over, forming a round ball. At roadsides and uncultivated fields. The tops of the soft and tender stems add flavour to vegetable dishes.

Ferula communis L.

III-V

Perennial bush with a thick, empty stem, huge leaves, similar to fennel. Large, long, round and yellow umbels. At limestone areas near residential areas. The core of the giant fennel is burned very slowly, while the cortex is intact. The Greek mythology says that god Prometheus used this plant to bring fire to the humans, as a gift. At its roots we may find delicious, large mushrooms (of the Pleurotus family).

8

Lecokia cretica
(Lam.) DC.

III-V

80cm
40cm

Perennial plant of south-west Asia, while its appearance of the island of Crete is unique in Europe. Many glabrous, trifid leaves, with dentate leaflets. Umbel with white to ochre-yellow flowers and fairly hairy fruits. At olive groves, trenches and rocky areas between bushes.

Aristolochiaceae:

• *Aristolochia cretica* **Lam.**

60cm
30cm

III-IV

Perennial, herbaceous plant, Asiatic in origin. Leaves 6.5cm, triangular, ovate with a heart-shape on the base. Flowers 5-12cm, with a cannular, arched brown-ochre corolla, widened above, covered internally with long, white hair, distended at base. At rocky and shady areas and on the roots of trees.

9

Aristolochia sempervirens L.

III-VII

C l i m b i n g
plant with very long stems,
leaves cordate up to 6 cm and
flowers brown-red externally and yellow internally, on long pedicels.
Fannel-shaped base, hairy mouth. At fences, lands with bushes and rocky areas.

Asteraceae:

Achillea cretica L.

IV-V

Plant with p e r e n n i a l rhizome and stems covered in thick down. Leaves 6-2cm, winged with numerous small leaflets. Small, white flowers, f o r m i n g beautiful umbels. At rocky areas and banks.

10

Anthemis chia L.

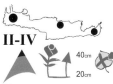

II-IV

40cm
20cm

The commonest of the daisies. Lanceolate leaves and capitulas up to 45mm in diameter, on long pedicels. Ligules larger than the disc, composed of very small, cannular, yellow, same height flowers. External bracts triangular, sharp and scarious, edges brown. At fields, olive groves, road-sides, in and around villages.

Asteriscus spinosus (L.) Sch,Bip = *Pallenis spinosa* (L.) Cass.

Annual or biennial plant with soft hair, woody base, branching stem, leaves spear-like, acute at tip. Capitulas 18-20mm, bright yellow, surrounded by pointed bracts-leaves, double than the dark yellow ligules. At heaths, roadsides and uncultivated fields.

30cm
20cm

IV-V

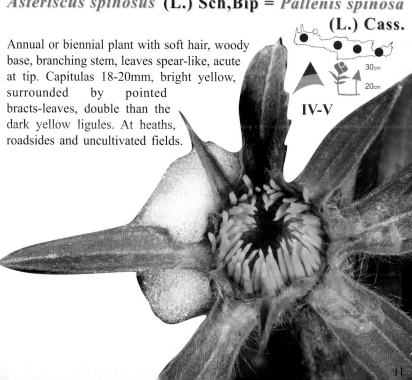

Centaurea argentea **L.**

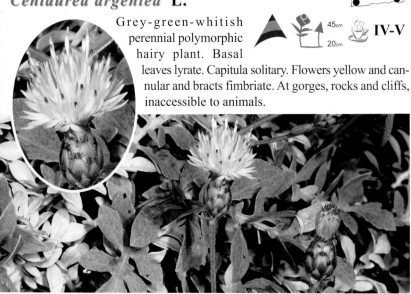

Grey-green-whitish perennial polymorphic hairy plant. Basal leaves lyrate. Capitula solitary. Flowers yellow and cannular and bracts fimbriate. At gorges, rocks and cliffs, inaccessible to animals.

45cm
20cm
IV-V

Centaurea raphanina **Sibth.& Sm.**

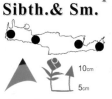

10cm
5cm

IV-VI

Perennial plant, practically stemless, with a radish-like perennial rhizome. Basal lobe with glabrous, whole, or lyrate leaves.

Capitulas without pedicel, with cannular, rosette florets. Hypanthium bracts with a spine. At rocky, uncultivated land.

12

• *Centaurea redempta* **Heldr.**

Perennial plant with erect stems, simple, or slightly branching, covered in thick, 50cm 30cm IV-VI
arachnoid hairs. Lower leaves stalked, pinnate. Round hypanthium, 30-40mm. Hypanthium bracts black, fimbriate, usually with a spine. Florets cannular, black-purple. In Greece, it is believed that the name of this plant ("Centaurea, the merciful one") comes from this black-purple hue of its flowers, since it's similarity to the blood of Christ the Savior. At limestone cliffs and rocks.

Cichorium intybus L.

Perennial plant, slightly hairy or glabrous, with a perennial rhizome. Leaves of the lobe usually lanceolate. Tall branching stem, with axillary capitula, up to 40mm, opening in the morning. Light blue ligule, with blue stamen. At cultivated and uncultivated fields, at roadsides. The fresh lobes and the tender leaves, raw, or boiled, make a wonderful salad.

V-VII

Chicorium spinosum L.

IV-V & VII-IX

Perennial, prickly genista. Stems short, branching from the base. Lobe with pinnately-dentate leaves, growing on the axilla of older branches. Soft leaves very delicious. Capitullas similar to cichorium intybus, though smaller, with less lingulae. Many years ago, the dried cichorium spinosum was used as a pitcher cap and for this reason the Cretans call it "pitcher-spine". At rocky areas to clay ground.

Helichrysum barrelieri (Ten,) Greuter = *H. stoechas* (L.) Moench

IV-VI

Perennial plant, with many stems and linear leaves, covered in white down. Ball-shaped capitulas, golden-yellow, surrounded by scarious bracts, forming dense corymbs on top of the stems. Particularly aromatic. At genista fields and rocky areas.

Lamyropsis cynaroides (Lam.) Dittrich

V-VI

Perennial prickly plant with arachnoid hair. Pinnately-lobed leaves with white hair along the veins, especially underneath. Capitulas 3-4cm, solitary, or grouped together on top of bare pedicels. Purple-pink cannular florets. At uncultivated and infertile areas.

Ptilostemon chamaepeuce (L.) Less.

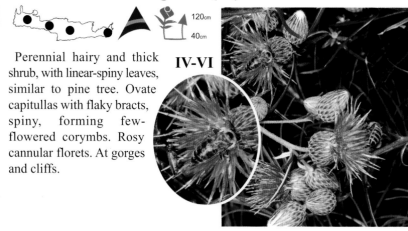

IV-VI

Perennial hairy and thick shrub, with linear-spiny leaves, similar to pine tree. Ovate capitullas with flaky bracts, spiny, forming few-flowered corymbs. Rosy cannular florets. At gorges and cliffs.

Steptorhamphus tuberosus (Jacq.) Grossh.

V

Perennial plant, occasionally branched, with nodular roots and a thick, milky sap. Lower leaves entire, or pinnately-lobed, upper entire. Capitulas with involucral bracts, reddish, glabrous. Yellow florets. At rocky areas and generally fallow and uncultivated fields.

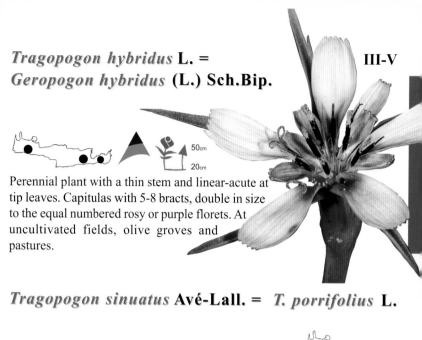

Tragopogon hybridus **L.** = *Geropogon hybridus* **(L.) Sch.Bip.**

III-V

50cm
20cm

Perennial plant with a thin stem and linear-acute at tip leaves. Capitulas with 5-8 bracts, double in size to the equal numbered rosy or purple florets. At uncultivated fields, olive groves and pastures.

Tragopogon sinuatus **Avé-Lall.** = *T. porrifolius* **L.**

Biennial plant with leaves branching, linear, pointy and wider at base. Large capitulas with rosy and violet florets and bracts larger than the peripheral florets. Following pollination, the bracts bend over. At fallow meadows and heaths. The whole plant, even the flowers, is edible.

III-V

90cm
30cm

Berberidaceae:

Leontice leontopetalum L.

II-IV

Biennial plant, erect, branching, green-blue. Leaves up to 20cm, bipartite or tripartite, with ovate entire leaflets. Raceme with 15 to 40 flowers at the axillas of the upper leaves. Flowers with 6 large sepals and 6 small petals, all yellow. At uncultivated and cultivated fields. The legend says that Ariadne, the daughter of King Minos, used the plant's fibres to make the famous "Ariadne's clew", with which she saved her lover's life.

Boraginaceae:

Anchusa azurea Miller = *A. italica* Retz.

III-VI

Beautiful, perennial, hairy plant with a thickly branching stem. Leaves up to 30cm, acute at tip and entire, lower ones stalked, upper ones sessile. The flowers can take many colours, from dark blow to bright red, lighter at the centre, 5 wide petals and linear sepals. At roadsides and abandoned fields.

Cerinthe major L.

Annual plant with large, sessile leaves, spathulate, full of whitish blotches. Flowers tubular, growing on short, long racemes, yellow, base usually dark purple. At cultivated and uncultivated fields, wastelands.

Myosotis incrassata Guss.

IV-V

Annual herb, covered in straight hair. Basal leaves ovate-lanceolate, up to 4cm. Stem usually branching. Corolla up to 3mm, light blue. At dry and rocky areas.

Onosma erectum **Sm.**

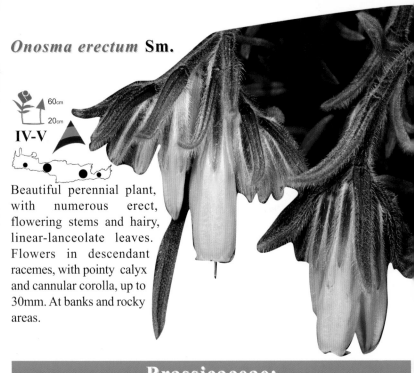

IV-V

60cm
20cm

Beautiful perennial plant, with numerous erect, flowering stems and hairy, linear-lanceolate leaves. Flowers in descendant racemes, with pointy calyx and cannular corolla, up to 30mm. At banks and rocky areas.

Brassicaceae:

Aethionema saxatile **R.Br.**

25cm
10cm

III-IV

Annual or perennial plant, glabrous, much-branched, with a woody base. Leaves oblong-linear and fleshy. Flowers with 4 small pink or purple petals, forming dense, long inflorescences. Its name, "aethionema" refers to the Greek words "aitho" (burn) and "nema" (string), apparently because following flowering, its stems look like they're burned. At cracks of rocks and rocky areas.

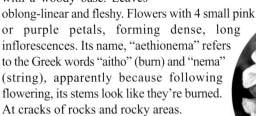

• *Allyssum baldaccii* Vierh. = *A. fallacinum* Hausskn

Perennial plant, hairy, much-branched, with almost all of his stems flowering. Many leaves oblanceolate up to 25mm, corrugated. Inflorescence corymb-like with many small yellow flowers. At uncultivated fields, roadsides, rocky areas.

60cm
20cm

V-VI

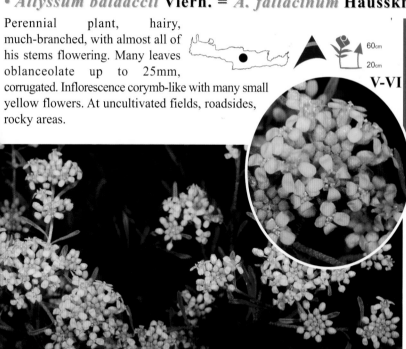

Perennial hairy herb with many small lobes, comprised of ovate-spathulake leaves, dentate at the edges. Spiny stem leaves. Flowers with 4 white petals up to 10mm double in size to the sepals.

Arabis alpina L.

35cm
10cm

IV-V

21

• *Erysimum raulinii* **Boiss.**

IV-VI

Biennial plant with a quadrangular and slightly winged stem.

Upper leaves large, oblong-lanceolate, up to 15cm, lower leaves forming a lobe. Yellow aromatic flowers in a dense long raceme. At genista fields and rocky banks.

Malcolmia chia **(L.) DC.**

III-V

Annual plant, slender, branching and hairy. Ovate-oblong leaves with a wedge-shaped base, entire or dentate. Both sepals saccate. Violet, pink and sometimes whitish flowers with 6-9mm petals. At cliffs, rocky areas and roadsides.

Mathiola sinuata (L.) R.Br.

III-IV

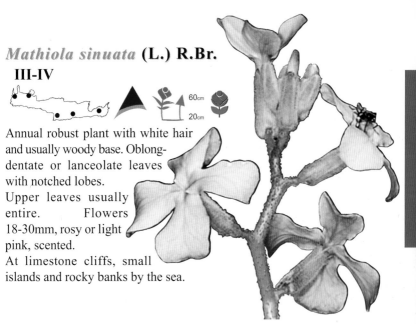

Annual robust plant with white hair
and usually woody base. Oblong-
dentate or lanceolate leaves
with notched lobes.
Upper leaves usually
entire.   Flowers
18-30mm, rosy or light
pink, scented.
At limestone cliffs, small
islands and rocky banks by the sea.

• *Thlaspi creticum* (Degen & Jàv.) Greuter & Burdet

IV-VI

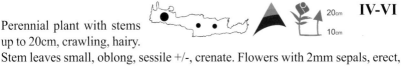

Perennial plant with stems
up to 20cm, crawling, hairy.
Stem leaves small, oblong, sessile +/-, crenate. Flowers with 2mm sepals, erect,
without saccate and white petals 6mm. At limestone rocky grounds.

Campanulaceae:

• *Campanula creutzburgii* Greuter

20cm III-IV
10cm

Annual hairy plant with branching stems, oblong-dentate leaves and a small corolla, tubular-cannular, violet. At rocky hills, banks, cracks of rocks by the sea.

• *Campanula pelviformis* Lam.

Biennial plant with erect stems, usually woody. Basal leaves ovate, sharp, hairy, dentate, stalked. Calyx with pointy lobes and corolla up to 40mm, blue-violet, occasionally white, broadly campanulate, swollen in the middle, divided at top into 5 triangular lobes, bending downwards. At crack of rocks and heaths.

50cm IV-V
15cm

• *Campanula tubulosa* **Lam.**

Biennial plant, hairy with a dichotomous stem, lower leaves stalked, oblong-ovate, dentate and upper leaves growing sessile. Flowers tubular up to 30mm, corolla always light blue-violet. Calyx with p o i n t y lobes, directed to the middle of the corolla. At cliffs, gorges and rocky banks.

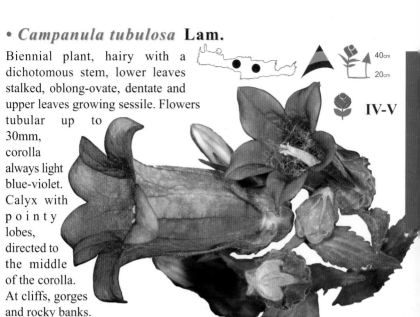

40cm
20cm

IV-V

Legousia pentagonia **(L.) Druce**

Annual plant, branching, with alternate leaves, lower ones obovate, stalked and the upper ones sessile. Flowers with a rotate, pentagonal, violet corolla up to 25mm in diameter. Hairy calyx with pointy lobes. At genista fields and rocky areas.

30cm
10cm

IV-V

Legusia speculum-veneris (L.) Chaix

30cm
10cm

IV-V

Annual hairy plant, much-branched. Small obovate or oblong leaves, with slightly curvy edges. Rotated corolla, violet, 16mm in diameter. The fruit contains numerous shiny seeds, similar to the broken looking-glass of Venus. At rocky areas and wastelands.

• *Petromarula pinnata* (L.) A. DC.

IV-V

Biennial plant with winged glabrous lobes and stems. Large leaves up to 30cm, pinnately-lobed or lanceolate, stalked, with oblong, dentate leaflets. Raceme-like inflorescence, with many light blue flowers. Corolla divided into 5 linear lobes, bending backwards. This plant is the unique representative of the species. At city walls, ruins, rocky areas.

Caryophyllaceae:

• *Dianthus xylorrhizus* Boiss. & Heldr.

IV-V

40cm
20cm

Perennial plant with dense branches, woody at base. Oblong-linear leaves. Usually 4 epicalyx scales, brown, ovate, pointed. Calyx 20-25mm. Petals 4-6mm, shiny, whitish, dentate. At rocks and rocky areas.

Paronychia macrosepala Boiss.

Perennial grass-like plant, markedly branching. Lanceolate, pointy grey-green leaves. Round inflorescences, surrounded by silver membraneous semi-transparent bracts, larger than the flowers. Green calyx. At rocky areas.

20cm
15cm

III-VI

• *Silene vulgaris ssp. suffrutescens*
Greuter Matthäs & Risse

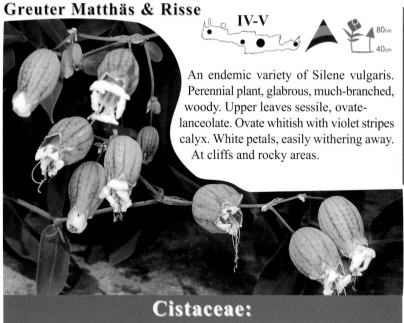

IV-V

80cm
40cm

An endemic variety of Silene vulgaris. Perennial plant, glabrous, much-branched, woody. Upper leaves sessile, ovate-lanceolate. Ovate whitish with violet stripes calyx. White petals, easily withering away. At cliffs and rocky areas.

Cistaceae:

Cistus creticus L. = *C. incanus ssp. creticus* Heywood

80cm
50cm

III-IV

Perennial aromatic, much-branched, dense shrub. Leaves ovate-lanceolate, curvy at edge, stalked, in opposite direction to the resinous, adenoid hair. Flowers up to 5-6cm in diameter, with 5 rosy-purple wrinkled petals and 5 ovate sepals. The plant secretes the resin laudanum. At sparse woodland and vegetation, at genista areas.

Cistus monspeliensis **L.** **III-V**

Perennial shrub, resinous with linear, sessile leaves. Flowers up to 30mm in diameter, with 5 white petals, bilobate on top and 5 sepals, the two external are smaller towards the base.

Cistus salvifolius **L.**

IV-V

Perennial shrub, hairy, with leaves 2-4cm, similar to the sage, ovate-elliptic, stalked, rough at base. Flowers up to 5cm in diameter, on long pedicels. White petals, solitary or grouped in 4 and 3 sepals. At sparse woodland, genista fields and heaths.

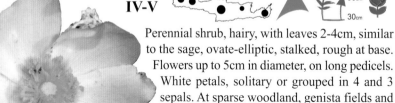

Convolvulus oleifolius **Desr.**

Perennial plant with a woody stem and silverish lanceolate- linear leaves  III-V & X-XI

similar to the olive tree. Funnel-like flowers, light-pink, up to 3cm in diameter, in long inflorescences. At rocky areas, genista fields, sandy banks by the sea, in small islands.

31

Crassulaceae:

Sedum hispanicum L.

Annual or biennial plant, grass-like, glabrous. Linear-lanceolate leaves,  glaucous-green. Flowers with 6 to 9 segments. White pointy leaves with a middle pink rid. At montane and sub-montane rocks.

15cm
07cm

IV-V

Dipsacaceae:

Knautia integrifolia (L.) Bertol.

IV-V

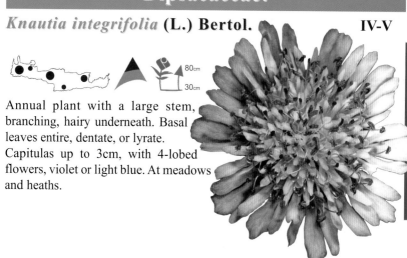

Annual plant with a large stem, branching, hairy underneath. Basal leaves entire, dentate, or lyrate. Capitulas up to 3cm, with 4-lobed flowers, violet or light blue. At meadows and heaths.

Lomelosia brachiata (Sm.) Greuter & Burdet

IV-V

Annual small, hairy plant with erect stem. Basal leaves lyrate or lanceolate, entire, up to 8cm. Capitulas light purple, up to 20mm, with few florets, surrounded by large bracts. At uncultivated fields and rocky areas.

Fabaceae:

• *Ebenus cretica* L.

120cm
50cm

IV-V

Small shrub with trifoliate or quinquefoliate leaves. Leaflets oblong- ovate, 15-30mm, silvery-haired. Deep red flowers, with hypanthium hairy bracts in dense hairy racemes. Corolla 10-15mm. At banks and rocky hillsides, usually in large, arresting colonies. In the past, people used them to fill in mattresses and pillows.

Lathyrus clymenum **L.**

Annual glabrous climbing plant, with winged stem. Leaves lanceolate, with wide leaf-like stipules. Lower leaves linear-lanceolate, upper with 2-4 pairs of leaflets and a broadened and winged tendril. Flowers 15-20mm, forming groups 1-5, standard red-dark purple and p i n k - v i o l e t wings. At olive groves, cultivated and uncultivated fields. In the past it was used as oat.

III-IV

Lupinus pilosus **L.** = *L. varius ssp. orientalis* **Franco & P.Silva**

III-IV

Annual hairy plant. Leaves with 7-10 oblanceolate, corrugated leaflets. Simple inflorescences in a raceme, with blue flowers whorled. Pod, with a white spot in the middle. At banks, olive groves and fallow meadows. The weeds of L. Albus (picture on the left) are used during the fast of Lend.

• *Securigera globosa* (Lam.) Lassen = *Coronilla*

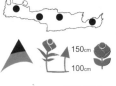

150cm
100cm

IV-VI

Perennial shrub-like plant. Leaves lanceolate with oblong glabrous leaflets. Numerous flowers on ball-shaped capitulas, up to 6cm in diameter. White petals and pod in rosy stripes. At banks of gorges, ravine and cliffs.

Spartium junceum L.

globosa Lam

300cm / 100cm · IV-VI

Shrub with grey-green, glabrous, erect, cylindrical branches, similar to b u l r u s h. Small, insignificant leaves. Inflorescence in very long racemes, aromatic flowers up to 25mm, in shiny yellow. At roadsides, heaths, abandoned fields. The stems were used for rope, baskets, brooms and shoes.

Tetragonolobus purpureus **Moench**

III-IV

Annual plant with soft hair. Leaves trifoliate with rhomboid leaflets and leaf-like stipules. Flowers 15-22mm, solitary, or in two, with a red-crimson pod and red-purple wings. At olive groves, cultivated fields and wastelands. Its fruits are edible.

Gentianaceae:

Centaurium erythraea **Rafn.**

IV-VI 30cm 10cm

Beautiful biennial plant, with a square stem, inter-branched. Basal leaves entire, obovate-elliptic and stem leaves pointy, reversed. Inflorescence in a dense corymd. Dark pink 5-lobed corolla. At rocky areas, banks and roadsides.

Geraniaceae:

Geranium lucidum L.

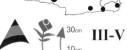

30cm
10cm
III-V

Small annual plant, erect or spreading. Orbicular leaves, shiny, green, flushed with red, dived up to the middle into 5 obovate-cuneate lobes.

Flowers usually in pairs with shiny pink obovate petals 8-10mm. At shady places, cliffs, rocks, walls and fences.

Geranium molle L.

Annual plant, extremely hairy, adenoid, spreading, grey-green. Basal leaves

40cm
20cm
III-V

up to 4cm, kidney-like, divided into 5-7 parts, cuneate, trilobate. Flowers purple-pink, 7-10mm with bilobate petals, larger than the sepals. At fields, rocky banks, roadsides, gardens.

Hypericum empetrifolium **Wild.**

III-V

Small perennial plant, diversiform (three sub-species), with stem erect, spreading, even herbaceous. Small linear leaves, pointy, in groups of three, with a white rid in the middle. Yellow flowers, usually red hued, 14-18mm, forming long bunches. Sepals with black marks on the edge. At rocks, roadsides, rocky banks, Mediterranean vegetation.

• *Hypericum jovis* **Greuter**

Small perennial shrub with  erect stems. Small leaves, linear, somehow rounded at edge, in groups of 3, without white rids. Few flowers, yellow, in sparse panicles. At cliffs and gorges of central Crete.

Hypericum perfoliatum **L.**

Perennial plant with an erect stem, usually glabrous with two characteristic prominent lines alength. Leaves shiny light blue, reversed, ovate-lanceolate, glowing. Flowers yellow, 16-26mm, in extreme panicles, with round, spotted sepals. At trenches, moist meadows and shady, rocky areas.

• *Hypericum trichocaulon* Boiss. & Heldr.

Perennial crawling plant, with many root-producing stems at knees. Leaves ovate-oblong, 5-14mm. Flowers with yellow petals, red near the stem and with smaller sepals with black spots. At genista fields, rocky areas, usually protected in between prickly plants.

Lamiaceae:

Lamium bifidum Cirillo

This is a plant, quite different than the rest of the Lamium family of Crete. Leaves slightly hairy, cuneate at base and rhomboid at top, slightly dentate, with a white-silverish rid in the middle. White flowers with some spots at lower lip, similar to Orchis Quadripunctata and with an upper lip bilobate, hairy. Was found at Mount Psiloritis on 05.05.2007, in a shrubbery of Berberis Cretica, maples and oaks and at Kakoptero of Chania on 05.03.2003.

Lavandula stoechas **L.**

A semi-evergreen, branching, aromatic shrub, with linear leaves, grey, hairy. Small flowers, bilobed, dark-violet, on top of dense spike. Its top with long-bracts corolla, light-violet, up to 50mm. At heaths, genista fields, rocky areas. Is used as a spice.

Phlomis cretica C. Presl

Small hairy shrub. Leaves lanceolate, stalked, velvet-like. Flowers yellow in dense whorls and calyx dentate with ciliates. At dry, rocky areas, oak forests glades and uncultivated fields.

Phlomis fruticosa L.

IV-VI

150cm
100cm

Large evergreen shrub, covered in white-grey down. Leaves completely covered in white hair beneath and green-grey above. Upper leaves sessile, lanceolate, rounded at tip. Lower leaves lanceolate-elliptic, stalked. Flowers yellow 23-35mm, in alternating dense whorls. At rocky areas, roadsides, heaths.

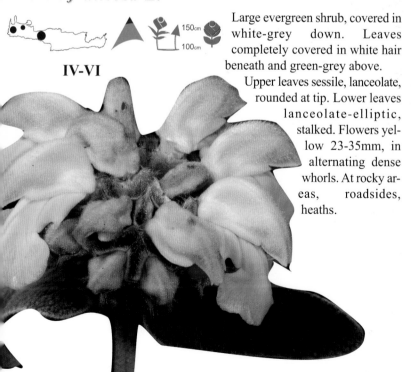

45

Small, very hairy shrub, with small leaves ovate-round, washy green. Flowers yellow 20-23mm, in less dense whorls. At rocky areas, genista fields, river beds and gorges.

Salvia pomifera **L.**

Perennial shrub, with large ovate, wavy, aromatic, velvet-like.  **V-VI**

Whorls with 2-4 flowers on the axilla of the upper leaves. Corolla 30-35mm, light blue, with neck white, bedight with blue-violet spots, upper labellum arched and lower labellum trilobite. At rocky cliffs, banks and pine forests. Makes a nice, aromatic tea.

• *Scutellaria sieberi* **Benth.**

IV-V

Plant with an evergreen rhizome, long stems, erect or spreading, leaves ovate, dentate, pointed 2-5cm. Flowers in dense, spike-like inflorescences.
Corolla white-cream, with upper labellum arched, trilobite and lower entire. The plant is covered in dense down. Cliffs, gorges and crack of rocks.

Linum bienne **Mill.**

Annual   or   biennial glabrous plant, often branching from base  onwards. Stems erect, slender, leaves small, entire, linear- lanceolate, alternating and flowers blue-red, with darker radiating stripes. Corolla radiating with 5 falling petals and five smaller, pointy sepals. At fields, genista fields, roadsides and sandy areas. Linseed oil is a product of its seeds.

III-V

50cm
20cm

Malva sylvestris L.

120cm
30cm

II-VI

Perennial or biennial plant, usually spreading, with a revolving rhizome. Leaves kidney-like, with 3-7 dentate lobes. Flowers in two, light pink-red, with darker rids. Petals 12-20mm, cuneate, bilobate and hairy, elliptic calyx lobes. Cultivated and uncultivated fields, roadsides.

Myrtus communis L.

IV-VI

Ever-green shrub, or small tree, with leaves ovate-lanceolate, pointy, coriaceous, adenoid beneath, with very aromatic essential oils. Flowers solitary on top of a large pedicel, with 5 white petals and many long stamens. Fruit, elliptic berry. Moist areas, banks of watercourses. Avoids limestone areas.

Orobanchaceae:

Orobanche pubescens d'Urv.

III-IV

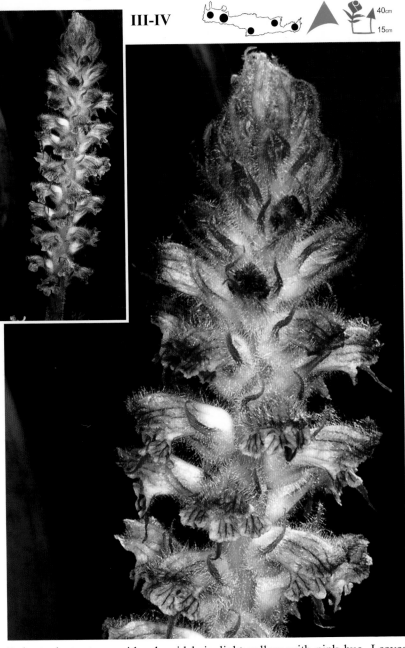

Robust plant, stems with adenoid hair, light yellow with pink hue. Leaves scale-like, oblong to linear, 10-25mm. Flowers in sparse raceme-like inflorescence. Corolla 10-20mm, light yellow with violet hue. Parasitic on Asteraceae, Fabaceae and Apiaceae.

Paeoniaceae :

• *Paeonia clusii* Stern & Stearn

90cm 40cm   IV-V

Perennial plant with reddish stems and glabrous leaves, multifarious with leaflets deeply divided into pointy lobes. Large flowers 7-10cm in diameter, totally white, rarely pinkish, beautiful. Almond-shaped fruits.

Papaveraceae:

Papaver rhoeas L.

Annual hairy plant, with green, pinnately - lobed    **III-V**

leaves. Beautiful flowers 70-100mm, in red-scarlet, often with a black blotch at base. 4 disc-like petals and black-blue anthers. Glabrous capsule. At cultivated and furrowed fields. Used in cooked vegetables and vegetable-pies.

Primulaceae:

Anagallis arvensis **L.**

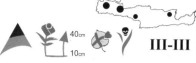

Annual or biennial plant, crawling or erect, with leaves ovate- lanceolate, reversed, glabrous. Flowers red, pink or blue, on equal-height, or shorter pedicels. Small hairs cover the periphery of the petals. Cultivated and uncultivated fields.

III-III

Lysimachia serpyllifolia **Schreb.**

IV-VI

Small plant with many stems and leaves reversed, ovate, pointy. Flowers 10mm, stellular, yellow, solitary, with a long pedicel at the axilla of the leaves. Capsule similar to glass ball. Its name ("Lysimachia" – defeat at battle) refers to the incompetence of the man, wounded at battle. At rocky areas.

Rafflesiaceae:

Cytinus hypocistis L.

Perennial bizarre plant, without chlorophyll, parasites on the Cistus family. Stems fleshy, like small nests. Leaves bract-like, red-carmine, turning into orange following flowering. Flowers yellow, or white, shiny, male at center and female on the periphery. The Greek name "hypokistos" is referred to the ancient botanist Dioscurides.

Rosaceae:

Prunus prostrata Labill.

Small deciduous, creeping shrub with crooked stems, which embrace tightly the rocks. The plant grows at the cracks of those rocks. Leaves ovate-elliptic dentate and flowers red-pink, almost without a pedicel. Berry red, bitter-sour. At rocky areas.

57

Sanguisorba minor **Scop.**

Perennial plant, greyish with usually hairy stems. Leaves lanceolate forming a lobe, with 3-12 pairs of ovate or elliptic, dentate leaflets. Flowers without petals, in ovate-round bunches, upper ones female with a reddish style and lower ones male with yellow anthers. Green sepals. Sides of fields, grassy areas. The word "Sanguisorba" means "blood-absorbent".

Rubiaceae:

Asperula pubescens (Willd.) Ehrend & Schőnb = IV-V *A. incana* Sm.

40cm
20cm

Perennial small hairy plant with angular stems. Leaves linear, pointy, in groups of 6, forming whorls.
Flowers white-pink with a long tube, in dense capitulas. At cliffs, rocky areas and banks.

Saxifragaceae:

Saxifraga chrysosplenifolia Boiss.

III-IV

50cm
10cm

Perennial herb with kidney-like leaves, dentate, +/- fleshy. Beautiful white flowers create sparse, corymd-like inflores-cences.
Corolla with 5 petals, 6-10mm, with red dots around base and 10 radiating anthers. At rocky areas and cracks of rocks. The name Saxifraga means "rock-crusher".

59

Verbascum macrurum Ten.

IV-VII

Biennial, tall, hairy plant, with large lanceolate leaves, 20-50cm, stalks-less. Many flowers, yellow in a very dense, spike-like inflorescence. At open banks, rocky areas and roadsides.

Veronica sartoriana Boiss. & Heldr.

10cm **IV-V**
05cm

Annual dwarf plant, with reversed leaves,
ovate-rhomboid, dentate, hairy, adenoid.
Corolla rotate, light blue, with 4 lobes, one of
them is different. At rocky areas and cypress forests.

Solanaceae:

80cm
30cm

III-V

Biennial or perennial plant, erect, with a heavy aroma, covered with adenoid-sticky hair. Leaves stalked, ovate, dentate. Corolla 30mm, cannular-campanulate, white-yellow, with 5 unequal round lobes, red or yellow throat and 5 projecting stamens. Found at old walls, ruins, debris and sides of roads. In Greek, Hyoscyamus literally means "pig's bean". It is unknown whether pigs eat it.

Hyoscyamus aureus **L.**

Biennial or perenni-
al plant, Asiatic ori-
gin (Mount Sina),
with adenoid, very sticky hair. Stems erect, or descendant, easy to break. Leaves
ovate-orbicular, lobular. Flowers golden-yellow, with a red throat and tube
30-45mm, in sparse racemes. Prominent stamens. Tubular calyx, hairy, with
triangular teeth. At city walls and old walls of houses.

60cm
20cm

II-IV

Styracaceae:

Styrax officinalis L.

A deciduous tree, with leaves ovate and hairy underneath. Flowers with a pedicel, white, scented, in small raceme-like inflorescences. Corolla campanulate with 5-7 lanceolate lobes. Calyx cap-like. The myth says that Rhadamanthus, the brother of the Cretan king Minos, transported this plant, when he moved to Boeotia. At cool locations, trenches and river banks. Unique representative of the entire family in Europe.

Thymeleaceae:

Daphne sericea Vahl.

III-V

A beautiful, ever-green, much-branched shrub. Leaves lanceolate, +/- fleshy, hairy underneath. Scented, silky flowers, in apical bunches. Corolla pink-violet, surrounded by small, soft bracts. Bright red berry. At rocky areas and genista fields.

65

Valerianaceae:

• *Valeriana asarifolia* Dufr.

Plant with a perennial rhizome and annual stems, robust, erect and glabrous. Basal leaves kidney-like, stem leaves pinnate. Apical, head-like, dense inflorescence, with white or pink flowers, with a button. At rocky areas and genista fields.

Violaceae:

• *Viola cretica* Boiss. & Heldr.

III-IV

III-V

Perennial herb with stolons. Leaves stalked, cordate, with flat dents. Violet flowers with a button. At cool places, watercourses, fountains, shady rocks.

67

Arum concinnatum Schott

A plant with nodular rhizome. Leaves 15-35cm, spiny, green,  with white rids, appearing during autumn. Large spadix, yellow-green sometimes with red hue and yellow spathe, shorter, with male flowers on top and female beneath. Red berry. At fields and olive groves, usually in numerous colonies.

rum creticum **Boiss. & Heldr.**

The most robust and beau-
iful plant of its family in
urope. Leaves blade-
ike, dark-green, 8-15cm, appearing at autumn. Spadix 10-18cm, half-open,
right-yellow. Spathe yellow, standing out of the spadix. It's said that the
roma of the flower is sweet and pleasant. At rocky areas, genista fields, or among
parse trees and in between piles of rocks.

III-V

50cm
20cm

69

• *Arum idaeum*
Coustur. & Gand.

IV-V

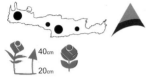

Small pretty plant with spiked leaves, unusually large. Spadix 5-8cm, white, seldom white-green and spathe shorter, blacks-purple. At rocky areas with genista and shrubs.

Dracunculus vulgaris Schott

IV-V

130cm
50cm

A striking plant with a thick nodular rhizome and a robust blotted, flowery pedicel.
Long-stalked leaves multifarious, divided into 10-15 linear-lanceolate parts, with white blotches. Minute flowers at base of a huge, dark-purple spathe. Spadix 25-40cm, dark-red, velvety externally greenish.
Inflorescence with nauseating smell.
At roadsides, abandoned fields and river banks.

A strange variety of this plant is found at the south banks of mount Psiloritis at altitude  from 500 to 1000m. Spadix greenish-white, or green with violet lips and spathe dark purple above and green-white beneath, or totally yellow above and green-violet beneath.

Iridaceae:

• *Crocus sieberi ssp. sieberi* Gay

III-VI

This is the most large and beautiful crocus of Crete. More than 5 leaves, with a light hue rid in the middle. Flowers with a white perianth and wide, violet, external fasciation on 3 of the 6 sepals, yellow throat and anthers and yellow-orange spots, entire. At rocky areas and fields where the snow melts.

Gladiolus italicus Miller

Plant with bulb-like rhizome, robust stem, 3-5 gladiate leaves and 6-16

IV-V

flowers circa on a spike, purple-pink, up to 5cm long. Beautiful ornamental plant. The ancients referred to it as "jacinth". At cultivated and uncultivated fields, olive groves and meadows.

Allium neapolitanum Cirillo

70cm
20cm

III-IV

Bulbous plant with a triangular stem, 2-4 linear-lanceolate leaves, glabrous and spadix smaller than the flowery pedicel. Umbel sparse up to 10cm in diameter, with white flowers, cup-like or stellular, 15-20mm. At cultivated and uncultivated fields, olive groves and roadsides. Used in cooked vegetables and pies.

Allium nigrum **L.**

IV-V

100cm
40cm

Large bulbous plant with round stem. 3-6 leaves, a at base, wide, linear spiky, smaller than th stem.
Inflorescence dense umbel-like. Flower in stellular arrangement, whit or lilac, with a gree vain on the outside an a green-black ovary.
At cultivated an abandoned fields.

Asphodelus aestivus **Brot.**

120cm
50cm

III-VI

Perennial, powerful erect plant, with thick, spindle-shaped rhizome, cylindrical empty stem and leaves tape- and keel-like, grey-green, all at base.
Much- branched inflorescence with white flowers 20-30mm. Tepals with a brown-reddish central vain. At rocky, infertile areas, olive groves and abandoned fields, usually in large colonies, since it is non-edible. Edible bulb.

Fritillaria messanensis **Raf.**

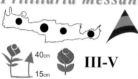

III-V

Perennial small plant, with a slender stem and leaves linear, whitish-blue, the upper 3 in a whorl. 1-2 purple-brown flowers, campanulate, with leaves slightly curved outwards at tip, checkers-like, with red-brown blotches and dashes and usually with a green stripe in the middle. At sparse forests, meadows, rocky areas and genista fields.

Muscari comosum **(L.) Mill.**

III-V

Perennial bulbous plant with a leafless stem and 3-7 basal linear leaves, up to 20cm long. Raceme with fertile flowers, small, pineal, brown-white, with creamy-yellow dentates at the lower part and barren, blue-violet on top, forming a plume.
The bulbs are a hard-to-find appetiser.

Ornithogalum nutans **L.**

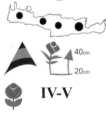

IV-V

Perennial herb with 4-6 tape-like, corrugated leaves, with a midvain. Silver-green flowers, wide, bell-like, 30-35mm, fallen, beautiful. At fields, genista and alpine meadows.

• *Tulipa bakeri* **A. D. Hall**

III-IV

Perennial plant, glabrous, leaves oblong-lanceolate, corrugated, assembled about base. Tepals 4-5cm long, yellow at base, white at centre and pink at the edges, though mainly pink. Yellow anthers. Scattered all over the Omalos plateau of Chania.

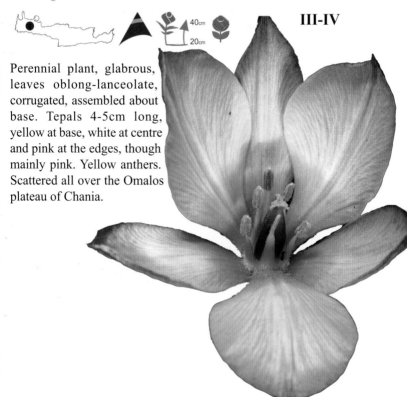

• *Tulipa doerfleri* Gand.

Perennial plant, glabrous, with linear-lanceolate leaves, corrugated and  flowers solitary, sometimes in two. Tepals 3-4cm, pointy, red-carmine, usually yellow hued. Black-red anthers. Ten years ago, this fair tulip, found at Amari and Ious Plain, was common, though today is unfortunately endangered.

Tulipa saxatilis Sieber ex Spreng.

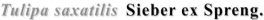

III-V

Though many report similarities to Tulipa Bakeri, we'll just say that this tulip is found everywhere, except the Omalos plateau and the high-lands of Chania. Obviously, the only difference is the colour of the anthers (in Tulipa Saxatilis they are brown-black). At rocky areas, banks of watercourses and uncultivated fields.

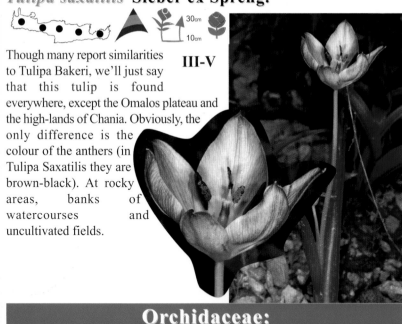

Orchidaceae:

• *Cephalanthera cucullata* Boiss. & Heldr.

V-VI

Perennial plant, looking like a herb, with hood-like leaves and bracts. Dense inflorescence with 5-24 white or whitish-pink flowers, half-open. Small-medium labellum with a concave underlip and an overlip bedight with yellow-ochre projections. The plant looks like a baby in its cradle. At forests with oaks, maples, cypresses and pines, in between rocks and pebbles.

Dactylorhiza romana (Sebast.& Mauri) Soó

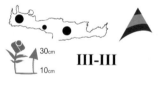

III-III

A plant with lanceolate unblotted leaves, most of them forming a lobe. Inflorescence cylindrical with yellow-whitish, or red- violet, or intermediate hue flowers. Long button, facing upwards. At alkaline to acid grounds, with sparse forests, or vegetation.

• *Himantoglossum samariense* C.& A. Alibertis

V-VI

Plant with brown-green stems and 5-8 large leaves. Inflorescence sparse, with 12-20 flowers, with a trilobate lip and long mid-lobe 50-80mm, twisted, brown-red, bifid, strap-like. At sparse forests and outskirts of forests.

Ophrys apifera Huds.

Robust plant with leaves usually dried out during flowering season. Inflorescence, 3-8  flowers in flashy colour, white, green, yellow, violet, purple, pink and red. Small-medium labellum, trilobate, velvety. This is the only ophrys which performs autogenesis. At benches, moist fields, genista fields and sparse forests.

Ophrys cretica (Vierh.) Nelson *var. bicornuta*

25cm
10cm
III-VI

A plant with a sparse inflorescence, 2-8 flowers. Sepals greenish-pink, petals triangular, usually brownish-red, small-medium labellum, trilobate, dark brown to black-purple, with enlarged side-lobes, pointy, horn-like. It's supposed to be a "moody" plant. At uncultivated for many years fields, among genista and abandoned olive groves.

Ophrys episcopalis Poir. =
O. holocerica ssp. maxima (H.Fleischm.) Greut.

Robust plant, 3-8 flowers. Pink sepals and small, triangular, same-colour sepa-  45cm 15cm **III-IV**

ls. Large entire labellum, velvety, brown, with two small horny-like projections at base. Shield diversiform and colourful. Large appendix. The plant looks like bishop's orphrey canonicals. At abandoned vineyards and olive groves.

Ophrys heldreichii Schlechter

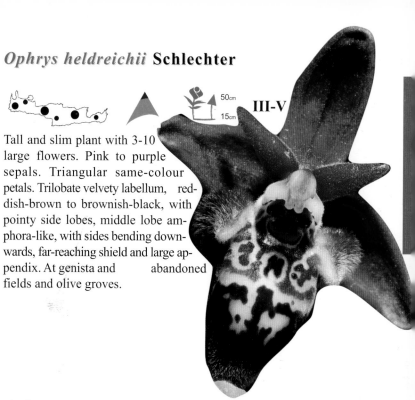

III-V

Tall and slim plant with 3-10 large flowers. Pink to purple sepals. Triangular same-colour petals. Trilobate velvety labellum, reddish-brown to brownish-black, with pointy side lobes, middle lobe amphora-like, with sides bending downwards, far-reaching shield and large appendix. At genista and abandoned fields and olive groves.

Ophrys omegaifera H. Fleischm.

Short plant with 2-5 flowers. Greenish sepals and green petals, brown at tip. Small-medium labellum, uncut at base, with a knee bend ascendant, light brown. Bending side lobes, as the middle one. Shield at top forms a colourful omega shape (ω). At benches, abandoned olive groves and sparse forests.

II-IV

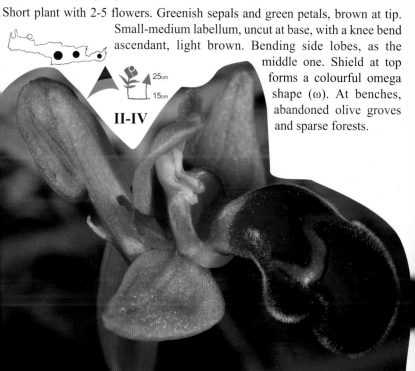

Ophrys tenthredinifera **Willd.**

The O. tenthredinifera of Crete is recently divided into 3 subgroups: O. Leochroma, O. Dictynnae and O. Villosa.  Dense inflorescence with 2-8 flowers. Large colourful sepals, whitish, yellowish, pink, purple and violet and small, same-coloured, hairy, triangular sepals. Small-medium labellum, entire, hairy, dark-brown to reddish, with glabrous edges and appendix emerging from a tongue. Genista fields, rocky areas and sparse forests.

II-V 35cm 10cm

Orchis anthropophora (L.) All. =
Aceras anthropophorum (L.) W. T. Aiton

A plant with a much-flowered, long inflorescence. The flowers are like a hanged man.  III-V

Small-medium labellum, trilobate, greenish-yellow, red at tip, without a button and that's why its previous name was "Aceras" (buttonless). Side lobes vibriform, like the edges of the midlobe. At sparse forests and genista fields.

Orchis boryi **Reich.**

A plant with a sparse  inflorescence, 3-15 flowers, opening off-beat, first the upper ones and then the lower. Sepals and petals red-purple, with green rids internally and dark violet externally. Small-medium

l a b e l l u m , t r i l o b a t e , usually in light colour, bedight at centre with two rows of violet dots. Long and slim button. At alpine meadows and sparse forests.

Orchis collina **Banks & Sol.**

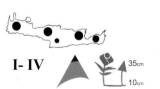

I- IV

Robust, with a brown-violet stem on the upper part. Relatively dense inflorescence, 4-15 flowers, supported by purple-violet bracts. Sepals brown-violet or greenish. Same colour petals. Labellum entire, colourful, red, pink, whitish-green, folded in a shape of a Chinese roof. Fleshy button. At genista fields, uncultivated land and generally grassy areas.

Orchis elegans **Heuffel** = *O. palustris ssp. elegans* **(Heuffel) Nyár**

A tall body plant, with a purple-violet stem and large leaves up to 25cm, approaching the base of the much-flowered inflorescence (15-20 flowers). Flowers red-violet, with an almost entire labellum, spotted centre and a totally white base. Horizontal button. At almost flooded fields by the sea. Endangered because of the destruction of its biotopes.

120cm
60cm
IV-V

Orchis italica Poir.

III-IV

40cm
15cm

Robust plant with a lobe
consisting of 5-10 large lanceolate
leaves, dark green, with violet
spots, or unspotted. Dense
inflorescence, with many pink,
lilac, or purple flowers. Medium
size labellum, humanlike, deeply
trilobate, bedight with dense lilac
or purple spots. Side lobes
lanceolate, aristate and midlobe
with a corpuscle, in between the
secondary aristate lobes. At genista
fields, meadows and olive groves.

Orchis laxiflora
Lam.

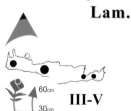

60cm
30cm **III-V**

Tall, with a violet stem on
the upper part and 3-8 leaves,
linear-lanceolate, corrugated.
Bracts violet on top. Sparse
inflorescence with many
dark-violet flowers. Medium
size labellum, trilobate,
almost folded vertically in
the middle, with a white,
unspotted centre. Side lobes
dentate and midlobe almost
non-existent.   Large,
arcuate button. At moist
areas,   meadows   and
swamps.

Orchis papilionacea ssp. alibertis
G. & H. Kretzschmar

tem higher than the sub-species
sp. heroica, with 4-10 flowers,
maller on top.

IV-V

Uniform colouring at all populations. Dome red, or pinkish-red, with purple rids.
Medium size labellum, concave, fan-shaped, whitish-pink with dark purple spots
nd lines and dentate edges, folded upwards. At genista and abandoned fields.

Orchis pauciflora **Ten**

III-IV

Plant with spotless leaves and
scarious, yellowish bracts. Sparse
inflorescence with 4-15 large, yellow
flowers. Sepals and petals
ochre- yellow to white. Medium size
labellum, trilobate, almost folded in
two alength, shiny yellow with
purple spots at centre. Button long,
cylindrical. At genista fields and
rocky areas.

• *Orchis prisca* **Hautz.**

IV-V

Plant with a red-violet stem on top. Sparse inflorescence with 5-10 flowers pink to lilac. Darker side sepals with dark green centre be-dight with red spots. Medium size labellum, trilobate, coloured lighter at centre with purple-lilac dots. Side lobes falciform and midlobe spathulake. Short button, pineal, arcuate. At sparse forests, genista fields and rocky areas.

Orchis simia **Lam.**

III-V

Robust, with 2-6 large ovate-lanceolate leaves, up to 20cm. Dense inflorescence with many flowers, flowering conversely. Medium size labellum, monkey-like, deeply trilobate, with a white centre, bedight with purple puffs. Side lobes linear-vibriform and midlobe divided into 2 vibriform lobes. Cylindrical button. A genista fields, rocky areas and banks, relatively moist.

Orchis sitiaca **(Renz.) Delforge**

Robust, with grey-green leaves, shiny, spotted and sparse inflorescence with 3-16

flowers, whitish to violet, green hue. Small-medium size labellum, cuneate, trilobate, coloured lighter at centre, bedight with two lines of dots, looking like a landing aisle and a deep mid ridge. Lobes facing downwards. Long button. At Genista fields, sparse forests and pastures.

Gramvousa

SUMMER

Acanthus spinosus **L.**

Perennial plant with simple, erect bracts and leaves reversed,

80cm
30cm
IV-VI

pinnate, with spiny dentates, surrounded at base. Inflorescence in dense spike with large leaves, sessile and spiky bracts. Corolla pinkish-white, with entir upper labellum and trilobate lower. At rocky areas, abandoned fields and oliv groves.

Acer sempervirens **L.**

This is the first and only time that we'll speak of fruits and not flowers.

During summertime, this maple, which never drops its leaves, turns red, owing to the wings of its fruits. The plant is beautiful. At mountains, usually in company of oaks and cypresses.

Mesembryanthemum crystallinum L.

80cm
20cm
V-VII

Perennial herbaceous plant, branching, covered in shiny papillae, filled wit
water, reminding the magic of crystals. Leaves alternate, ovate, fleshy, juicy
slightly cymose. Flowers up to 3cm in diameter, with vibriform, white-silver
petals. At sandy and rocky beaches. The soft leaves are edible. In the pas
people used to make soda drinks.

Eryngium maritimum

Perennial beautiful pale blue plant,  VI-VIII
with erect branching stems at upper part. Coriaceous leaves, with
3-4 spiky dentates. Blue flowers in capitulas, with diameter up to 3cm, surrounded
by spiky bracts. At sandy beaches.

Pimpinella tragium ssp. depressa (DC.) Tutin

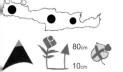

VI-VIII

Perennial plant, creeping, dwarf, with thick, woody rhizome and brittle stems. Leaves pinnate with leaflets up to 5mm, ovate, deeply dentate. Umbels with 3-7 rays and white, beautiful, microscopic flowers. At rocky areas, cracks of rocks and in between spiky shrubs.

Nerium oleander L.

500cm
150cm

V-VIII

Evergreen impressive shrub with leaves in groups of 2-3, lanceolate, pointy, wit
a strong skin membrane, which make the plant sun- and draught-resistan
Red-pink flowers. Corolla funnel-like, with 5 round lobes and adenoid sepal
Acute smell and bitter taste. At river beds and roadsides.

• *Carlina corymbosa ssp. curetum* (Heldr. ex Halácsy) Rech.

Perennial, with pinnately-lobed leaves, spiny and solitary capitula 12-18mm, with cannular florets, surrounded by

VII-VIII

50cm
30cm

spiny bracts, brown-yellow, that look like ligule, supported by blond, spiny leaves-bracts. The plant was named after Karolus Magnus (Charlemagne), for it's said that he treated his soldiers, who suffered from plague, using a similar plant. Dry and infertile areas.

Carlina corymbosa ssp. graeca (Boiss.) Nyman

Perennial plant, in the same family as the previous one, larger and with more branches, with leaves

60cm
20cm
VII-IX

pinnately-lobed, spiny and solitary capitula, up to 30mm. Capitula bracts in bright yellow and supporting leaves narrower and with smaller spines. At genista fields and rocky areas.

• *Centaurea idaea* **Boiss. & Heldr.**

V-VIII

Biennial plant, much-branched, with winged bracts and pinnate leaves, forming a lobe. Bracts leaves entire. Capitula with yellow cannular flowers and yellowish bracts with a large spine, up to 30mm, with a white down in between them. At rocky areas and cracks of rocks.

• *Cirsium morinifolium* **Boiss. & Heldr.**

VII-VIII

Biennial plant with a large body, which stands out among the many herbaceous alpine plants, presented in 2 varieties. The one seen at Mount Lefka Ori of Chania has white flowers, almost un-branched, found at high altitude, the other at Mount Psiloritis of Rethimnon is much-branched, taller and wider, with violet

flowers, found at lower altitude. Leaves pinnate, spiny, glabrous on top and hair underneath, like the Morina persica.

• *Crepis sibthorpiana* **Boiss. & Heldr.**

Herbaceous plant, with hairy, pinnately-lobed leaves and capitula up to 20mm. Florets ligule-like, yellow with red gleams on the outside. Named after the great British botanist John Sibthrop, for his work "Flora Graeca". At rocky areas and piles of rocks.

10cm
05cm

VI-VIII

Cynara scolymus **L.**

V-VII

120cm
50cm

This is a variety of C. Scolymus. Tall, robust plant with large, pinnate, spiky leaves, huge capitulas, 10-20cm, with blue or purple-violet cannular florets and ovate bracts, grey-green with a hard spine at the edge. Cultivated at fields and gardens. More delicious than the gentle artichoke C. Scolymus with bracts and without an apical spine.

Echinops spinosissimus **Turra**

Perennial with a branching
stem. Leaves pinnate with
prickly lobes.

100cm
50cm

V-VII

Round capitulas with cannular florets, light blue to blue-violet, surrounded by
light green firm, spiny bracts. Named after the Greek words "echinus" (sea urchin)
and "opsi" (appearance), because of its spiny capitulas. At rocky areas, roadsides,
sandy beaches.

Helichrysum microphyllum (Willd.) Cambess. = *H. italicum ssp. microphyllum* (Willd.) Nyman

40cm
20cm **VI-VIII**

Branching, hairy, aromatic plant, with small, linear leaves and ovate capitulas in dense corymbs. Tiny cannular florets, surrounded by grey-yellow bracts. At rocky areas, sparse forests and genista fields.

• *Lactuca alpestris* Gand.= *Scariola alpestris* (Gand.) Greut., Matthäs & Risse

Spreading plant, branching, with light-blue, pinnately-lobed leaves and many capitulas, consisting of 4-5 ligule-like, yellow florets, with a con-cave, den-tate top.

10cm
05cm
VII-X

• *Onopordon bracteatum ssp. creticum* Franco

150cm
100cm
V-VII

Biennial plant with a robust grey-green stem. Pinnate leaves with many spines and dense hair underneath. Capitula up to 70mm in diameter, with dark red cannular florets and with robust, spiny, greenish-violet bracts. Named after the Greek words "onos" (donkey) and "pordi" (fart). At infertile, rocky areas.

Onopordon tauricum **Willd**

Biennial, green plant with winged stems, glabrous, pinnately-lobed leaves up to 25cm and round capitulas up to 70mm in diameter. Pinkish-red, ligule-like florets and spiny bracts, the upper ones ascendant and the lower ones descendant. At uncultivated fields and roadsides.

150cm
100cm
V-VI

Heliotropium hirsutissimum **Grauer**

V-IX

50cm
30cm

Annual spreading to ascendant plant, branching, with stalked, ovate, elliptic, grey-green leaves. Stems covered in grey or yellowish hair. White flowers, up to 6mm in diameter, forming raceme-like inflorescences. At cultivated fields, fallow meadows, roadsides.

Campanulaceae:

Campanula aizoides Zaffran ex Greuter

40cm
15cm
VI-VIII

Biennial erect plant, with a robust stem, spathulake, corrugated basal leaves and pointy, sessile stem leaves. Flowers up to 15mm, in a branching inflorescence, with a small, light-blue corolla and calyx with pointy lobes. Its Greek name means "the never-dying". At cliffs and rocky areas.

Capparaceae:

Capparis spinosa L.

Perennial much-branched shrub, divided into 2, difficult to differentiate sub-species, ssp. rupestris and ssp. spinosa. Coriaceous, wide, ovate, glabrous leaves and flowers solitary, on a long pedicel, with 4 white petals, 4 green sepals and many long, radiating, pink-violet stamens. At rocks near the sea, abandoned fields, ruins and wastelands. People make "vinegar-caper" from its flower buds.

Caprifoliaceae:

Lonicera etrusca Santi

V-VIII

V-VII

Small, much-branched, climbing shrub, with oblong-elliptic, glabrous leaves up to 8cm, the upper ones in two, stuck at base. Scented flowers, white-yellowish, up to 45mm, forming bunches on a long pedicel.

Double-labellum corolla with long stamens. At rocky banks, fences, sparse forests, Mediterranean vegetation.

Sambucus ebulus

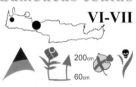

VI-VII

Perennial woody shrub, with a bad smell and bitter, unpleasant taste.
Lanceolate, dentate leaves. White flowers with 5 pointy petals in large umbels, 5-16cm in diameter. At roadsides, trenches and fences, usually in large colonies.

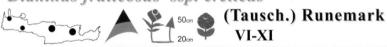

Caryophyllaceae:

• Dianthus fruticosus ssp. creticus

(Tausch.) Runemark
VI-XI

Small, woody shrub with linear, coriaceous leaves, rounded at tip. Scented flowers with calyx up to 22mm, sub-calyx scales 10-20 pointy, petals up to 10mm, dentate, pink, hairy at base and 10 stamens. At cliffs and rocky areas.

Dianthus juniperinus ssp. bauhinorum
(Greuter) Turland

Perennial woody plant, closely packed at base, with linear, spiky

leaves and robust, flowering stems, with more than 3 scentless flowers. Petals up to 10mm, dentate, light to dark pink, with rids and a red-dark pink circle at corolla center. At rocks and cliffs of Mount Yiouchtas of Heraklion. 7 sub-species of D. juniperinus have been identified on the island of Crete.

• *Dianthus juniperinus ssp. aciphyllus*
(Sieber ex Ser.) Turland

Perennial woody plant, with linear, sharp leaves. Robust flowering stems.

60cm 30cm

VI-VII

Flowers with pink, dentate petals, bedight with light to dark pink spots a lower half, which form a second, smaller corolla. At cliffs and upright banks

Silene variegata (Desf.) Boiss. & Heldr.

VI-VIII

Perennial plant with short stems and fleshy, grey-light blue, ovate-spathulake leaves. Grey-violet calyx with 10 rids. Red-brown petals, deeply bipartite. At rocky areas and piles of rocks.

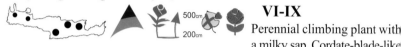

Calystegia sepium (L.) R. Br.

  500cm 200cm

VI-IX

Perennial climbing plant with a milky sap. Cordate-blade-like leaves. Flowers white, solitary, large up to 5cm, funnel-like, surrounded by two bracts, covering the calyx. The flowers open in the daylight, even with the full-moonlight and close in cloudy weather. At riverbanks and moist areas by the sea.

Convolvulus arvensis L.

 **IV-VIII** 100cm 10cm

Perennial plant with thin stems, sometimes climbing and blade-like leaves. Funnel-like flowers up to 20mm in diameter, white, pink or bicoloured, scented, solitary or in two. Common at fields and gardens.

Cuscuta sp. **Ten.**

40cm
20cm

VII-VIII

Parasitic plant with vibriform stems, embodied with plunger-like footstalks, which embrace the host stems and suck out the nutrients. Brown stems and small flowers, pink-violet at center and white at edge, forming round inflorescences. The Ancient Greeks believed the plant was the hair of the Nymphs and devils. At rocky areas, on spiky shrubs.

Ipomoea imperati **(Vahl) Griseb.**

100cm
20cm

VII-X

Perennial plant, with crawling or climbing stems and big roots. Fleshy leaves, alternate, oblong, entire or with 4-5 lobes. Funnel-like flowers, white, with a yellowish throat, 50-60mm, usually solitary. At sandy beaches, just above sea level.

• *Lomelosia albocincta* Greuter & Burdet = *Scabiosa albocincta* Greuter

 **VII-VIII**

Perennial woody shrub, with entire leaves, wide, elliptic, green, white at the edges (this is where its name "Albocincta" comes from). Pedicels of inflorescences 3-40cm, capitulas 4cm in diameter and beautiful, violet flowers. At cliffs and rocky southern areas.

Sixalix atropurpurea (L.) Greuter & Burdet = *Scabiosa atropurpurea* L.

V-VII

Biennial plant with hairy, branching stems, leaves oblong to spathulake, the lower ones entire, stalked and the upper ones pinnately-lobed. Capitulas lilac to dark pink, 20-30mm, with external leaves two times larger than the internal. At dry areas, unculti-vated land, sandy areas by the sea.

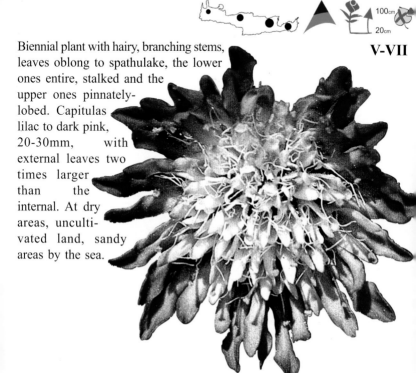

Astragalus angustifolius Lam.

50cm
20cm

VI-VIII

Perennial beautiful, pillow-like shrub, with many woody stems and 25-40mm dentate leaves, with 6-10 pairs of leaflets and a hard, needle-like back. Flowers 13-23mm, with a white pod and wings and bright pink carinas, 3-8. At rocky banks and clay, flat areas. A great refuge to plants avoiding being destroyed by animals and weather.

117

Astracantha cretica **(Lam.) Podlech**

40cm 20cm **VI-VIII**

Perennial, pillow-like shrub. Leaves 2-5cm, pinnate, with 6-7 pairs of linear-lanceolate leaflets, ending on a robust spine. Florets 1-12mm, in pairs on the axilla of the leaves, with a whitish-pink pod and light yellow wings and carina. At rocky, flat and clay areas. Refuge to plants avoiding being destroyed by animals and weather.

Cicer incisum **L.**

Perennial, crawling plant, with adenoid hair. Leaves imparipinnate, without a tendril, with 1-3 pairs of trilobate or pentalobate leaflets and ovate, dentate side-leaves. Dark violet butterfly-like flowers with a large pod. Edible fruits. At rocky areas and piles of rocks.

30cm **VI-IX**

Coridothymus capitatus (L.) Rchb
Thymus capitatus (L.)Hoff. & Link.

V-VII

Perennial genista, much-branched, aromatic, woody. Leaves linear, ciliate at base, adenoid, falling easily at draught. Flowers in dense, pineal inflorescences, with a bilobed light to dark pink corolla, up to 10mm and with prominent stamens. Bees fed with its flowers make the most delicious honey. At genista fields, rocky banks and sparse pine forests.

Mentha aquatica L.

VII-IX

Perennial plant, branching, aromatic, with leaves 30-90mm, ovate, sharp, dentate. Whitish-pink flowers, in dense whorls, forming an apical rounded capitula. Corolla with 4+/- same-length lobes. At moist areas, riverbanks and banks of lakes.

119

Mentha pulegium L.

Perennial, hairy, erect, very aromatic plant. **V-VI**

Small, grey-green, ovate leaves. Flowers whitish-pink, or lilac, in sparse many-flowered, round whorl. The name, "Pulegium", which comes from the Latin world "pulex" (flea), was given to the plant because of its insect appalling qualities. At moist areas, trenches and flooded land during winter. People use it to make a wonderful tea.

• *Nepeta sphaciotica* P.H.Davis

Perennial plant, erect, with not many branches, hairy, with a thick down. Leaves ovate, cordate at base, dentate. Flowers in apical many-flowered whorls, forming a spike. Corolla 12-15mm, light blue with red marks. While found at the north side of Mountain Svourichti, the plant is one of the rarest natives of the island.

VII-VIII

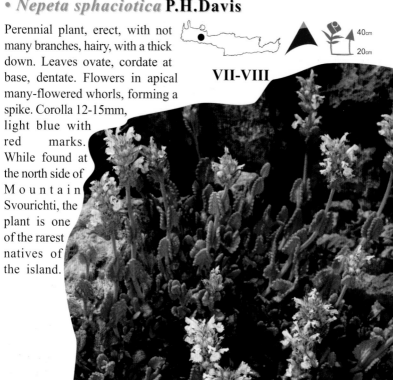

• *Origanum dictamnus* **L.**

VI-VIII  30cm 10cm

Perennial, much-branched, aromatic plant. Leaves 13-25mm, orbicular-ovate, covered in dense hair. Erect, hairy spikes, with few flowers.

Corolla reddish-pink, with projecting stamens, supported by large, reddish bracts. Quoted often in Greek mythology, where it's said even Gods used it. At cliffs, gorges and rocky areas.

Satureja alpina **(L.) Scheele** = *Acinos alpinus* **L.**

20cm 10cm **V-VII**

Perennial, hairy, aromatic plant with crawling or ascendant stems. Small, elliptic, pointy leaves. Small flowers in small, apical bunches. Hairy calyx and violet, hairy corolla. Limestone and rocky areas, usually in between pointy plants.

Satureja spinosa **L.**

Perennial spiny genista, with small, lanceolate leaves, up to 10mm. Many flowering stems, with axillary flowers. White corolla with violet spots. The flowers are so numerous, that they create beautiful whitish-green pillows. At rocky, limestone areas.

VII-VIII

30cm
10cm

• *Scutellaria hirta* **Sm.**

20cm
10cm

V-VIII

Small plant, very hairy, with 10-20mm leaves, ovate-cordate, slightly dentate. Flowers whitish-pink, hairy, on the axilla of the upper leaves-bracts. At cracks and piles of rocks.

Sideritis syriaca L.

VII-VIII

Perennial, hairy, erect plant, with 10-60mm leaves, reversed, lanceolate. Inflorescences with 5-20 sparse whorls, with 6-10 flowers each. Corolla 9-15mm, yellow, with a double labellum, the upper one biolobed and the lower triolbed. At rocky areas, genista and cracks of rocks. A wonderful traditional Cretan tea is made from the plant, called "tea of the mountain".

Malvaceae :

Alcea cretica (Weinm.) Greuter

VI-VIII

Large perennial plant, with robust, erect stems, almost leafless, though very hairy. Leaves cordate-orbicular, with lobes. Large flowers, up to 9cm in diameter, axillary, almost sessile, dark pink, with a light coloured throat. At fences, roadsides and wastelands.

Onagraceae:

Epilobium hirsutum L.

Perennial plant with underground stolons, robust, wingless stems with soft hairs. Sessile leaves, reversed, oblong, lanceolate, slightly crenate. Flowers 15-35mm, dark to light pink, in raceme-like inflorescences, with 4 belly-ending petals, 8 stamens and 4 widened spots forming a cross. At trenches and riverbanks.

V-VII

Plumbaginaceae:

Acantholimon androsaceum (Jaub. & Spach) Boiss = *A. ulicinum* (Willd. ex Schult.) Boiss

30cm / 10cm — VI-IX

Perennial, spiny, beautiful, pillow-like genista. Thick, spiny leaves, 10-20mm. Flowering stems, short, with dark or light pink flowers and funnel-like, scarious calyx, looking like a flower, which remains on the plant after the petals have dropped and embellish it. At rocky, limestone banks and clay, flat areas.

Limonium sinuatum (L.) Miller

40cm / 20cm — V-VIII

Perennial, with hard hairs, pinnately-lobed leaves, on a winged lobe and stems. Compact, umbel-like inflorescence. Androgynous flowers, with a white corolla, falling easily, in a beautiful, funnel-like, blue-violet calyx. At sandy and rocky beaches. Its dried flowering stems make beautiful bunches.

• *Polygonum idaeum* **Hayek**

Perennial plant with a woody rhizome, leaves ovate-elliptic and few  white flowers with yellow florets. Always present as a herbaceous, stem-less plant because forager animals do not let it develop. It's said than animals, which eat it, have golden teeth. At clay areas and in and around Nida plateau.

Ranunculaceae:

Delphinium staphisagria **L.**

IV-VI

Perennial plant, robust, unbranched, very hairy. Leaves plamately lobed, with elliptic lobes, or pointy trilobate. Raceme-like inflorescences with dark blue to pink, beautiful flowers. Corolla with 5 exterior elliptic petals, 4 interior small, with nectar, many stamens and a short button. The dust of the seeds was considered to be a strong louse-killer. At uncultivated, rocky areas, river beds, ruins and roadsides.

Rubiaceae:

• *Asperula idaea* **Haláscy**

Perennial herb, with green or light blue stems, sparsely hairy. Leaves linear, 5-8mm, pointy. Dense inflorescence with pink flowers in bunches. Quadralobate corolla on a long tube. At cliffs, rocky hillsides and clay, flat areas, usually in between spiky shrubs.

VI-VIII

Scrophulariaceae:

• *Verbascum spinosum* **L.**

V-VIII

Beautiful, perennial genista, spiky, much-branched, with very small leaves covered in down and with many, yellow, solitary flowers in diameter up to 18mm. Yellowish-green, rounded puffs in varying size, covering the alpine surroundings of the Lefka Ori Mountains of Chania. At rocky areas, Mediterranean vegetation and clay flat surfaces.

Datura innoxia **Miller**

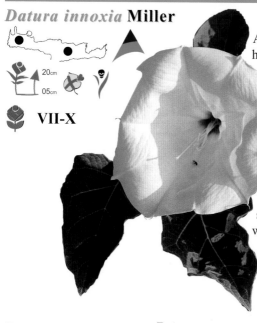

20cm
05cm

VII-X

Annual plant, erect, with a heavy scent, hairy, with ovate, spiny leaves.

Large flowers 11-19cm, white, sometimes violet hued, like a trumpet. Funnel-like corolla with 10 lobes, which dies out easily.

Extraordinary capsule, large up to 70mm, ovate, spiny, skewed. A weed, which is very toxic. At ruins, debris and wastelands.

Origin: central America

Datura stramonium **L.**

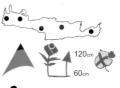

120cm
60cm

IV-VIII

Annual plant, completely glabrous, with an unpleasant smell and erect stems. Leaves stalked, large, dentate. Flowers solitary, axillary, up to 12cm long, white, trumpet-like. Angular calyx, at 2/3 of the length of the corolla. Fruit ovate, spiny, 10-15mm long.

At cultivated and uncultivated fields and roadsides. Very toxic. Origin: South America.

129

Verbenaceae:

Vitex agnus-castus L.

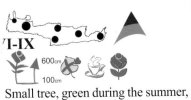

'I-IX

Small tree, green during the summer, smelling like pepper and robust, flexible branches. Leaves reversed, long-stalked, palmately lobed with lanceolate parts. Apical inflorescences, branching with many scented flowers in whorls. Double-labellum corolla, blue-violet, pink or white with 4 projecting stamens. Black fruit at the size of pepper. At riverbanks. Alleviates sexual desire.

Agavaceae:

Agave americana L.

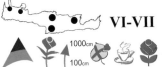

VI-VII

Plant with lobe consisting of huge lanceolate leaves 100-200cm, fleshy, dentate, spiky at edge, with an apical, black, thick spine. Flowers once in 10-15 years and produces a fascinating woody flowering pedicel up to 10m high, in a shape of a chandelier, with many 7-9cm scented, yellow-green flowers. Then, it dies out. Near villages and at roadsides. Mexican origin.

Alisma plantago-aquatica L.

100cm
40cm

VI-IX

Perennial plant, aquatic, with large, lanceolate leaves, glabrous, floating or underwater. Leafless stem, raceme-like. White flowers with 3 petals, semi-round, dentate at edge and many anthers. At standing waters or currents.

Mesara - Asterousia

AUTUMN

Asclepiadaceae:

Periploca angustifolia Labill.

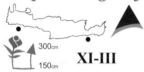

XI-III

300cm
150cm

Erect shrub, with reversed leaves, linear, glabrous, up to 3.5cm long. Inflorescences with not many flowers. Quinquelobate corolla, radiating, with dark pink-brown lobes, surrounded by a greenish-yellow side-corolla quinquelobate too, with convoluted lobes and white center. At sandy areas, in between Juniperus Phoenicea, at islands Chrysi and Gavdos.

Asteraceae:

?Aster squamatus (Spreng.) Hieron.

Annual plant with linear-lanceolate leaves and symmetric, panicle-like

X-XI

50cm
30cm

inflorescences. Capitulas with ligule-like florets, blue-violet when they are stil buds (i.e., externally), and white, when they open. At salty areas by the sea Origin: central and South America.

Aster tripolium L.

70cm
20cm **XI**

Annual plant, branching, glabrous. Leaves lanceolate, slightly fleshy. Panicle-like inflorescence with many, beautiful flowers. Capitulas with a yellow disc and ligule-like florets, light blue or dark red, up to 20mm in length. At moist areas by the sea.

Atractylis gummifera L.

30cm
10cm **VII-X**

Perennial plant, herbaceous, stem-less, with long leaves, oblong, spiny, surrounding a solitary, extraordinary capitula, up to 70mm in diameter. Florets cannular, pink-lilac, turning to white when mature. Bracts less extraordinary than the ones of Carlina. The milky sap, which is secreted from around the head, was used as a chewing-gum. At uncultivated, rocky areas.

Galatella cretica Gand. = *Aster creticus* (G.) Rech

40cm / 20cm — X-XI

Perennial plant, with thin, erect stems. Leaves lanceolate, alternate. Flowering capitulas in long, round bunches, with cannular flowers, yellow, or red-dark red, beautiful, with 5 lobes, reversed outwards and a sessile, very prominent ovary. At rocky and limestone areas and genista fields.

Convolvulaceae:

Ipomoea indica (Burm.) Merr.

500cm / 200cm — VIII-XI

Perennial, foreign, tropical plant, acclimated on the island. Leaves ovate-cordate, entire or trilobate, with ovate, pointy lobes. Large, funnel-like flowers, up to 60cm in diameter, blue-purple, with a lighter throat and 5 star-like rids. At creeks, gardens, fences and generally moist areas.

Euphorbiaceae:

Euphorbia dimorphocaulon P. H. Davis

IX-XI

20cm
10cm

Genista, spreading to erect, branching, with young, glabrous stems, or with tiny hairs. Leaves in 3-4, up to 8mm in length. Light-pink flowers, 3-3.5mm, like small bells, aromatic, in long, inflorescences with many leaves. Prominent anthers. At rocky, limestone hillsides. Ornament to the autumn landscape.

Ericaceae:

Erica manipuliflora Salisb.

60cm
20cm

VII-XI

Small plant, glabrous, with hardly any leaflets and panicle-like inflorescence. Flowers in 2-3 at the edge of each pedicel, small but beautiful. The cyanthiums (the flowers of Euphorbia) are comprised of a special receptacle, containing the male and female parts, surrounded initially by 4 greenish-brown semi-circular glands and following by bracts. At rocky and uncultivated areas.

Fabaceae:

Ceratonia siliqua L.

Dioecious, evergreen tree with leaves  pinnate, imparipinnate. Leaflet ovulate-elliptic, fleshy, 30-50cm. Flower self-growing, very small, without a corolla, creating extraordinary designs, best seen with a magnifying glass. Long ago, the seeds of its fruit, otherwise called "carats" (+/-200mg), were used as a measurement of the weight of gold.

IX-XI

300cm
100cm

VII-X

Small tree with glabrous stems, usually reddish and leaves large, lanceolate, up to 30cm. Raceme-like inflorescences, with small, petal-less flowers, but with 5 pink-violet, beautiful sepals. At gardens, sides of fields and roadsides. Origin: North America.

139

Primulaceae:

Cyclamen graecum Link *ssp. candicum*

Perennial plant with huge nods
up to 25cm in diameter and
self-sown rhizome. Cordate leaves, 4-10cm, reddish underneath, dark green wi
silver designs on top. Corolla with 5 white petals, with auricles at base and dar
pink-violet throat. At rocky areas and cracks of rocks.

Cyclamen graecum Link *ssp. graecum*

This is a similar plant,
slightly more robust, with
silver leaves, green at edge
and pink-violet flowers with a
darker throat. At similar areas.
The Ancient Greeks used to call it
"turtle" because of its nods.

Ranunculaceae:

Ranunculus bullatus L.

Perennial small herb, hairy, with a branching stem and all the leaves at base, stalked, orbicular-ovulate, dentate. Solitary flowers, 18-26mm, yellow, smelling like the violet on leaf-less pedicels. 5-12 petals and many stamens. At genista fields, banks and generally rocky areas.

X-XI

20cm
10cm

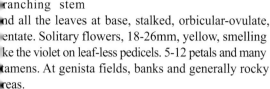

Solanaceae:

Mandragora autumnalis Bertol.

   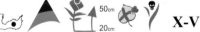

X-V

50cm
20cm

Stem-less plant, with perennial stake-like rhizome, usually divided, sometimes anthropomorphous. Leaves on a lobe, large, stalked, wavy at edge. Flowers pineal on pedicels, with 5 violet petals, white or reddish. Fruit, berry, up to 3cm, similar to a tiny melon. There are quite a few myths surrounding this plant, which has analgesic and hypnotic qualities. Cultivated and uncultivated fields, roadsides.

Amaryllidaceae:

Narcissus serotinus L.

IX-XI

Small daffodil of the autumn, with a thin stem, cylindrical leaves, which appear after flowering and 1-2 small flowers, no more than 30mm in diameter. Secondary corolla, very small, or-angey. At heaths, moist and rocky areas.

Pancratium maritimum L.

   **VIII-X**

Bulbous plant with a robust, widened stem. Light blue, tape-like leaves, dry during flowering. White flowers up to 15cm, scented, with 6 uniform linear-lanceolate sepals, secondary trumpet-like corolla, dentate at edge and six stamens. Black and very light like fruit, like coal, floating at surface, while the waves distribute it all over the coast. At sandy areas by the sea. The Minoans loved it.

Sternbergia lutea (L.) Ker. Gawl.

IX-XI

Perennial plant, looking like the saffron. 3-9 leaves, dark green, very long, c o r r u g a t e d, 8-15mm width, appearing sim ultaneously with the yellowish-gold-en flowers 40-50mm long. Ovate-elliptic teals, 7-15mm wide, joined at base and rounded at edge. 6 yellow anthers. At rocky areas, in be-ween dried plants.

Sternbergia sicula Tineo ex Guss.

IX-XI

A plant, looking like the above, but thinner and more common. Leaves with a white tape at middle, up to 5mm wide, appearing after flowering. Long tepals, 4-8mm wide. At rocky areas and in between Pinus Brutia and genista.

143

• *Biarum davisii* Turbill.

Perennial, bulbous, small plant, completely scentless, strange, beautiful and rare. Leaves ovate-elliptic, fleshy appearing after flowering. Cream spadix, 3-5cm long, brown-dark pink hued barrel-like base and helmet-like top. Spathe red-dark red, thin, like a tongue appearing out of the spadix. Used in abortions. At rocky areas and pastures.

IX-X

Biarum tenuifolium (L.) Schott

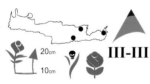

III-III

Perennial, bulbous plant, short, diversiform. Narrow leaves, long, linear, 10-20mm wide and wavy edges, appearing before or after the dark brown-chocolate spadix, 8-30cm long. Spathe larger than the spadix. At rocks, rocky areas and Mediterranean vegetation.

Iridaceae:

Crocus boryi Gay

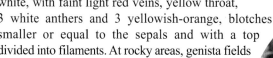

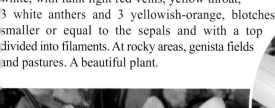

Perennial, stem-less plant. Leaves (3-7), linear, with a white mid-line. Scentless flowers, totally white, with faint light red veins, yellow throat, 3 white anthers and 3 yellowish-orange, blotches smaller or equal to the sepals and with a top divided into filaments. At rocky areas, genista fields and pastures. A beautiful plant.

X-XI

Crocus cartwrightianus Herb.

X-XII

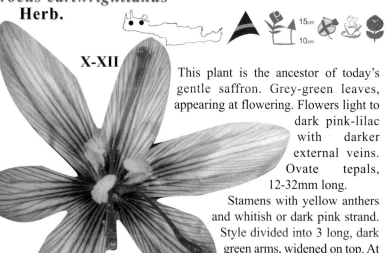

This plant is the ancestor of today's gentle saffron. Grey-green leaves, appearing at flowering. Flowers light to dark pink-lilac with darker external veins. Ovate tepals, 12-32mm long. Stamens with yellow anthers and whitish or dark pink strand. Style divided into 3 long, dark green arms, widened on top. At rocky areas and genista.

145

Crocus laevigatus **Bory & Chaub.**

Perennial crocus, with 2-4 narrow leaves with a  **IX-XI**
white, central tape, appearing simultaneously with the flowering. White scented flowers, with large, violet, external veins. Tepals 11-30mm long, dark orange throat, white anthers on top of orange strand and orange, branching style equal, or larger to the stamens. Common at genista and rocky areas.

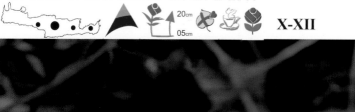

Similar to C. Cartwrightianus, which grows only at lower altitudes and at the district of Chania. Its shorter blotches and its darker colours are not characteristics, capable for differentiation between the two species. Though, the fact that this species isn't seen at the Lefka Ori mountains, or throughout the district of Chania, while is seen on the rest of the island, suggests that this is indeed a different species.

Crocus tournefortii **Gay**

Similar to C. boryi and is seen +/- on the same  areas. The sole difference is its colour (pinkish-violet). Same throat, anther and blotches. At rocky areas with genista and non-solid cliffs, at Vai palm-forest

Liliaceae:

• *Allium callimischon ssp. haemostictum* Stern

Perennial, small plant with corrugated, linear leaves, dry during flowering. The 7-10mm white tepals with dark-red spots (Haemostictum = blood-spotted) and the black anthers make it beautiful. At rocky areas, sides of fields and cracks of rocks, where there are no goats.

IX-X

Allium chamaespathum Boiss.

IX-X

Perennial, bulbous plant with narrow, tubular-corrugated leaves up to 4mm wide and round umbel up to 45mm. Light green flowers. Like all Alliums, there is a strong scent of garlic about it. The flowering in the midst of autumn is an evidence of eternal life. At rocky areas and banks.

• *Colchicum cretense* **Greuter**

Short plant with 5-8 leaves, appearing after flowering and pinkish-violet to white flowers with dark pink stripes. Tepals up to 20mm, linear-lanceolate, rounded at edge and stamens yellow with brown anthers. At rocky areas and pastures.

Colchicum cupanii **Guss.**

Beautiful short plant with leaves usually very wide and large, up to 15cm, present during flowering. 1-5 flowers, red-dark pink or white pink with stripes.
Narrow elliptic tepals, 10-25mm in length, dark-pink anthers and yellowish-white style. At rocky areas.

XI-XII

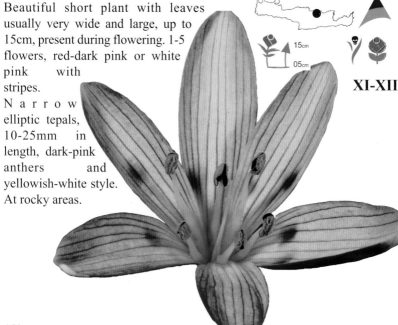

Colchicum macrophyllum B.L. Burtt

A plant with many large and wide leaves (up to 30x14cm), with parallel folds, appearing at spring. The flowers make their appearance during autumn, which are extraordinary in size and beauty. Lanceolate tepals up to 80mm, pink with dark-pink spots, like a mosaic. Brown-yellow anthers with white strand. At fertile, uncultivated fields, acorn forests and olive groves.

Colchicum pusillum Sieber

This is the smallest of the Colchicums of Crete, difficultly distinguished to C. cretense. Very narrow leaves, usually appearing after flowering. Flowers very small, pink or white, up to 4 on each bulb, with yellow or yellowish-brown anthers. At rocky banks, genista fields and clay, flat areas.

05cm
03cm

X-XII

Charybdis maritima = *Urginea maritima* (L.) Bake

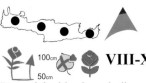

100cm
50cm

VIII-X

Perennial with a huge bulb up to 18cm in diameter, basal leaves lanceolate (100x10cm), appearing after flowering and apical, dense, raceme-like inflorescences with more than 50 flowers. White stellular tepals with green or dark pink veins and green anthers. Charming! At meadows, genista fields and rocky areas. Despite the fact that its Greek name means "by-the-sea", this plant is seen only above 1000m altitude.

152

Spiranthes spiralis **Koch.**

Thin plant with a hairy, grey-green stem. Lobe consisting of 5-7 leaflets, appearing during or after flowering, by the stem. Inflorescence relatively sparse, spiral with 6-25 small greenish-white flowers. Labellum small up to 6mm, yellowish-green, with frilled edges, just like icy snowflakes. At olive groves, pastures and sparse pine forests.

IX-XI

30cm
10cm

Avo Symi

Apocynaceae:

Vinca major L.

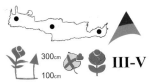

300cm
100cm

III-V

Evergreen plant with crawling or climbing stems, their edges easily forming rhizome. Ovate-lanceolate leaves, reversed, green, shiny. Flowers up to 50mm in diameter, blue-violet on a long pedicel. Corolla with 5 rounded lobes, forming a spiral. At riverbanks, garden-sides and moist areas. A spring forerunner.

Asteraceae:

Bellis annua L.

 15cm
10cm

II-IV

Annual small plant, glabrous or slightly hairy with short, erect stems. Ovate to spathulake leaves, lower ones stalked. 5-15mm capitulas, with tubular florets yellow at center and with a line of ligule-like, white florets, in dark pink hue externally, at periphery. At meadows and moist areas.

Bellis perennis L.

II-IV

30cm
10cm

Perennial plant with a basal lobe. Obovate or spathulake leaves, hairy, stalked. Leaf-less flowering stem. Capitulas up to 30mm in diameter, with a yellow disc and many white ligules with red spots externally. At cool areas, meadows, grass and acorn forests.

Carduncellus caeruleus (L.) C. Presl.

III-V

50cm
20cm

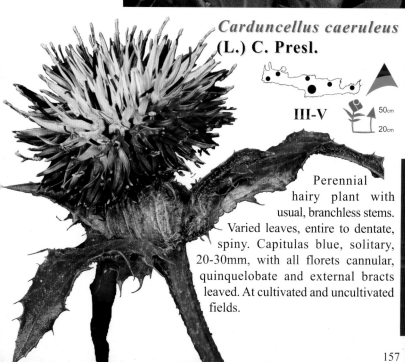

Perennial hairy plant with usual, branchless stems. Varied leaves, entire to dentate, spiny. Capitulas blue, solitary, 20-30mm, with all florets cannular, quinquelobate and external bracts leaved. At cultivated and uncultivated fields.

Filago pygmaea **L. =** *Evax pygmaea* **(L.) Brot.**

Annual dwarf plant, with a grey down. Leaves on a lobe, long, up to 15cm in length. Capitula yellowish-brown, in dense, small bunches up to 35mm in diameter. All floret cannular. At open, dry areas and rocky cliffs.

III-IV — 05cm / 02cm

Glebionis coronaria = *Chrysanthemum coronarium*

Annual plant with glabrous, branching stems and leaves double-pinnate. Large capitulas up to 60mm in diameter, with yellow cannular and ligule-like florets, dark-yellow or white. Common a uncultivated fields and wastelands. Traditionally, on May 1st people make garlands and necklaces.

III-V — 100cm / 40cm

Boraginaceae:

Echium plantagineum L.

Biennial plant, hairy. When fully blossomed takes the form of a cupola or pyramid. Leaves ovate-lanceolate, large, with robust rids. Funnel-like flowers, 10-30mm, initially red, then blue-purple or dark pink, with 2 out of the 5 stamens projecting. At uncultivated fields and sandy areas.

70cm
20cm
II-IV

Lithodora hispidula (Sm.) Griseb.

Much-branched, woody genista. Leaves lanceolate, coriaceous,  with thick hairs. Small flowers up to 10mm, funnel-like, quinquelobate, ligh blue-violet. At cracks of rocks, rocky banks and genista fields. African origin

Brassicaceae:

Aurinia saxatilis (L.) Desv. = *Alyssum saxatile* L.

II-IV

Perennial branching plant, with branched, lanceolate lower leaves and stalked upper leaves. Flowers forming long branching bunches. Bright yellow 4-7mm corolla with 4 bilobate petals. At cliffs and rocky areas.

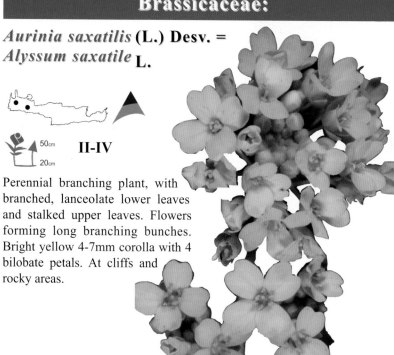

Brassica cretica Lam.

Perennial plant with fleshy leaves, light blue-green, 10-15cm and white or yellowish-white flowers on a long, branching, flowering stem. This ancestor of today's cabbage used to be a difficult to find appetiser. At cliffs and rocks, away from the menace of goats.

80cm
40cm

III-IV

Cakile maritima Scop.

Annual, herbaceous plant, fleshy, glabrous. Grey-green leaves, pinnate, with  unequal lobes. Pink, violet or white flowers in dense racemes with petals 5-14mm long. Sepals with a hump. At sandy beaches.

Lutzia cretica (L.) Greuter & Burdet = *Alyssoides cretica* (L.) Medik.

Much-branched with erect or ascendant stems,    covered in greyish down. Small, obovate or oblanceolate leaves. Petals 4-5mm slightly bilobate on top. Buttons disc-like, hairy. At cliffs and rocky banks.

Malcolmia flexuosa (Sm.) Sm.

Annual plant with fleshy, ovate-elliptic leaves. 35cm 10cm **II-IV**
Petals 12-17mm long, pink or violet with darker rids, two-coloured throat, yellow-white and slightly biolobate top. At rocky and sandy areas by the sea.

Caryophyllaceae:

Silene colorata Poir.

Annual plant, with erect stems, hairy at base and 40cm 10cm **II-IV**
small, lanceolate leaves. Pink beautiful flowers, 12-18mm, in sparse bunches of -4, with petals deeply bilobate and cannular calyx with reddish rids, distended on top. At sandy areas, usually by the sea, creating beautiful flower-beds.

Silene succulenta **Forssk.**

I-IV

Perennial plant, with thick, woody rhizome and many, sticky, hairy stems. L e a v e s oblanceolate, fleshy. Calyx slightly distended at middle, with parallel rids and flowers 15-20mm. Petals bilobate, white or pink, opening after sundown, or with cloudy weather. African in origin, settled on sandy areas at the south coast of Crete and on the islands of the Libyan Sea.

Crassulaceae:

Sedum litoreum **Guss.**

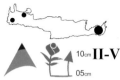

10cm **II-V**
05cm

Small, annual, fat plant with lanceolate-spathulate leaves, yellow flowers with linear-pointy leaves and almost equal sepals. At rocks and cliffs up to alpine zone.

Cucurbitaceae:

Bryonia cretica L.

Dioecious plant, hairy, climbing, with tendrils

ke the vineyard. Palmately lobed leaves, up to 10cm long, with white spots. mall, white-green flowers with darker veins. Males adenoid in hanging anicles and females in small bunches, on different plants. Red berries. Used to e cultivated for its medical qualities. At fences, near shrubs and olive roots.

Euphorbiaceae:

Euphorbia characias

L.

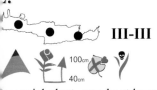

III-III

Perennial plant, woody at base, with robust stems and inear-lanceolate leaves, light lue, 13cm long, in dense rrangement. Long inflorescence vith an apical 10-20 rays umbel nd some at axillas of the upper eaves. Cyanthiums with dark ed-black glands and triangular, oncave bracts. At rocky areas.

Euphorbia dendroides L.

Beautiful small tree, glabrous, with a milky sap and candlestick-like branches. Leaves 25-65mm, lanceolate, falling easily during draught. 5-8 rays umbels, with yellow cyanthiums and same-colour rhomboid bracts. At rocky and infertile areas, creating large colonies.

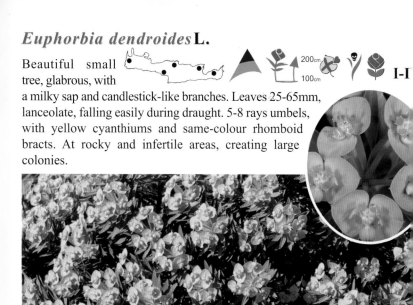

Euphorbia helioscopia L.

Small, annual plant, glabrous, with yellow-green, ovate leaves, beautiful 5-ray umbel and bracts just like the leaves. Dioscurides says its flow is always looking at the sun (Helioscopia = "looking-at-the-sun"). At crops a wastelands.

Euphorbia sultan-hassei
trid, Bentzer, Bothmer, Engstrand & M.A. Gust.

100cm
20cm

II-IV

uperficially similar to E. endroides. Actually, the florescence, the flowers nd the whole arrangement totally different from lant to plant. Seen only at me cliffs and gorges at the uth-west of Crete.

Fabaceae:

ecurigera securidaca(L.) Degen & Dörfl. = *oronilla securidaca*

30cm
20cm

II-IV

Annual plant, glabrous, with pinnate leaves with 4-7 pairs of leaflets. Leaflets long-oblong, sharply cut at edge. Capitulas with 4-8 yellow flowers, butterfly-like, 8-12mm long, on long pedicels.

At cultivated and uncultivated fields, near rivers and water supply channels.

167

Geraniaceae:

Erodium cicutarium (L.) L'Hér.

II-IV

Annual plant, diversiform, herbaceous, spreading, usually heavy scented. Leaves pinnate or pinnately-lobed. Pink to dark pink petals, sometimes white, the two of them slightly larger and with a black spot at base. At cultivated and uncultivated fields, roadsides, sandy and rocky areas.

Globulariaceae:

Globularia alypum L.

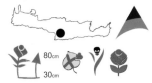

II-V

Perennial much-branched plant, always green. Small, hard oblanceolate leaves. Flowering capitulas up to 30mm in diameter, with tubular, blue-violet flowers and many spiky bracts. Double labellum corolla with bilobate upper labellum and trilobate lower labellum. At genista fields and sandy hills.

Lamiaceae:

Prasium majus L.

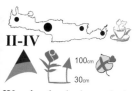

II-IV

100cm
30cm

Woody shrub, irregularly branching, glabrous. Ovate-lanceolate leaves with cardate base and dentate edges. Whorls with 1-2 flowers, 17-23mm, white or light lilac. Bilobate corolla with upper labellum arched and lower trilobate. Hairy calyx. Used during sauté cooking. At rocky banks between shrubs.

Salvia verbenaca L.

60cm
30cm

II-VI & IX-XI

Perennial plant with square stem, covered in adenoid hair. Large leaves with rids, pinnately-lobed with a long stalk at base and sessile on stem. Flowers 6-10mm, in sparse whorls. Dark blue or dark violet corolla.
At roadsides, rocky areas and wastelands.

Glaucium flavum Grantz

Biennial or perennial plant, slightly hairy with fleshy, light blue, pinnate leaves the upper ones slightly crenate. Extraordinary, golden-yellow flowers, 55-75mm solitary, sometimes with petals with an orange spot at base. Falciform capsule up to 20cm long. Beaches with sand, pebbles or rocks.

Cyclamen creticum **(Dörfl.) Hildebr.**

erennial plant with a ...odular rhizome. ...ordate leaves with ...ngular edges, which appear before flowering, similar to cissus. Solitary flow-...rs, white or slightly pink, on bare pedicels. Corolla 15-25mm, without any ...rojections at base. At cool, shadowy areas, forests, riverbanks and ...editerranean vegetation.

171

Primula vulgaris Hudson

30cm
10cm
III-IV

Perennial, hairy, short, with lobe leaves up to 15cm, entire, ovate, whitish-green with vivid rids. Beautiful, scented flowers, whitish-yellow, entire, on a long, bare pedicel. Corolla with 5 biolobate petals on top. Underneath chestnut and plane trees, at moist banks with ferns, nearby rivers.

Ranunculaceae:

Anemone coronaria L.

40cm
20cm
XII-IV

Annual plant with tripartite, stalked basal leaves. Nodular leaflets. Stems with 2 flowers, surrounded by 3 bract-like whorled leaves, divided into short bands. Flowers with no sepals, up to 65mm in diameter, with 5-8 elliptic petals, red, blue, violet, cream or white and black stamens. The anemone fields are truly so charming!

Anemone hortensis ssp. heldreichii (Boiss.) Rech.

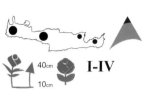

I-IV

Perennial plant with palmately lobed basal leaves, strikingly lobed and flowers with 12-19 petals, narrow, elliptic, white to pinkish-red and blue-purple anthers. At genista fields, olive groves and rocky areas.

Ranunculus asiaticus L.

Annual plant with bulbous rhizome, sim- **II-V** ple or branching stem and dentate, trilobate basal leaves. Large flowers with white, yellow, re or pink petals up to 70mm and a central bunch of black to dark-red stamens. Fascinating following morning dew or rain. At banks, genista and abandoned fields, always in uniform colonies.

Ranunculus creticus L.

I-IV

Perennial very beautiful plant, with erect, hairy branching stem. Large basal leaves up to 12cm, orbicular-kidney like, with dentate lobes and trifid stem lobes. Yellow flowers up to 30mm in diameter. At cliffs and rocky, shadowy areas.

Ranunculus ficaria ssp. chrysocephalus P.D. Sell

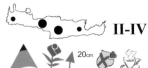

II-IV

Perennial plant, herbaceous, glabrous, robust, with slightly fleshy leaves, dark-green, ovate, cardate, dentate. Short stems with large, golden-yellow, shiny flowers, up to 40mm in diameter, consisting of 8-12 petals, which become white with time and 3 yellowish-white sepals. At olive groves, cultivated and uncultivated fields, relatively moist.

174

Fagonia cretica **L.**

Perennial crawling plant, glabrous, with angular, branching stems. Reversed,  trifoliate, stalked leaves, with asymmetric leaflets, spiny, like the stipules. Beautiful flowers up to 10mm, at axillas of the stipules, with 5 spathulate petals, dark pink to violet and many yellow stamens. At sides of roads and fields and rocky areas.

Amaryllidaceae:

Narcissus tazetta L.

Perennial, bulbous plant, with robust cylindrical stem and  equal size leaves, angular on the back. Descendant flowers with a heady perfume and a double corolla. External corolla with 8-22mm parts, spreading, white or cream, pointy and inner cup-like, yellow corolla. At moist or rocky areas. Unfortunately it's widely collected.

Arisarum vulgare **Targ. Tozz.**

Perennial plant, with ovate-blade-like, long-stalked leaves. Spadix 30-50mm long, green with dark pink lines, cannular base and arched upper part, hood-like. Wavy spathe, greenish on the upper part. At olive groves, forests, walls and rocky areas.

Iridaceae:

Gynandriris sisyrinchium (L.) Parl.

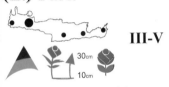

III-V

Plant with a bulbous rhizome, with corrugated leaves, dark-green, sometimes larger than the flowering pedicel and papyrus-like bracts in pairs, consisting of many flowers, 22-40mm, ephemeral, blue-lilac to violet. At genista and abandoned fields and rocky areas. Its name "Gynadriris" comes form "gyni" (γυνή=woman), "andras" (άνδρας=man) and "iris", referring to the reproductive system of the plant and its relevance to the iris.

Hermodactylus tuberosus (L.) Mill.

Plant with a bulbous rhizome, **II-IV** thin, with long green-grey leaves, linear, with a square section. Scented, solitary flowers, green-yellow, with dark brown-violet, sometimes yellowish-green, velvety external tepals, two times larger to the internal. At rocky areas, banks and fields.

Iris planifolia
(Mill.) Fiori & Paol.

I - III

Plant with a bulbous rhizome, with large, wide leaves (10-30mm), almost flat, green, shiny, in a fan-like arrangement, all at base. Flowers 1-3, blue-violet, with a long tube, 8-15cm, external tepals with a wing-like nail and central projection yellow, surrounded by blue-violet veins. Very small internal tepals, horizontal, dentate. At rocky areas and genista fields.

Iris cretensis
Janka

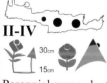

II-IV

Perennial cyme plant, with many linear leaves and short stems. Very beautiful flower with dark red petals, bedight at center with y e l l o w - w h i t e arresting designs. At genista fields and rocky areas.

179

Romulea bulbocodium (L.) **Sebast. & Mauri**

Bulbous plant with 3-7dark green leaves.
Beautiful flowers, white to lilac, usually green-violet externally, with
yellow throat and elliptic-pointy tepals, 2-35mm. The flowering
pedicel, the absence of a white line on the leaves and the absence of long, red
blotches, make this plant different to the Crocuses. At genista and uncultivated
fields and flat, clay areas.

II-IV

Liliaceae:

• *Androcymbium rechingeri* **Greuter**

I-II

Beautiful plant, almost branchless,
similar to Colchicum. Long, lanceolate, glabrous leaves, up to 15cm long and
flowers 3-5cm in diameter. Lanceolate tepals, white, with pink blotches. Yellow
throat and anthers. At sandy and rocky beaches.

Asphodelus fistulosus L.

II-IV

60cm
20cm

Perennial with many fleshy roots, linear leaves, all at base, cylindrical, cavernous, branching stem and r a c e m e - l i k e inflorescence, with white or pinkish flowers, 16-24mm. Tepals 12-14mm long, with brown or pinkish mid-rid. Rocky and sandy areas, field-sides and roadsides.

Bellevalia brevipedicillata **Turill.**

I-II

20cm
05cm

Small, bulbous plant with 2-3 basal leaves, wide, lanceloate, corrugated, wavy, up to 20cm long. Inflorescence with 9-25 small, six-parted flowers, white, cannular and g r e e n i s h - p i n k perianth edges. At rocky and sandy areas by the sea.

• *Bellevalia sitiaca*
Tzanoudakis & Kypriotakis

I-II

Similar to above, with only slight differences. This bellevalia seen in Sitia district is found at rocky areas and banks of gorges, not too close to the sea.

Gagea peduncularis
(J.& C.Presl. Pascher

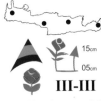

III-III

Small plant with stem covered in small hairs and linear, cardate leaves. Flowers 1-3, yellow, 10-20mm, with externally greenish tepals. At shrubs, genista fields and rocky areas.

• *Muscari spreitzenhoferi* (Heldr. ex Osterm.) Vierh.

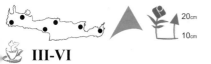

III-VI

Diversiform small plant, with wide and raceme-like inflorescence with cannular flowers, not many, barren, the lower ones many, fertile, brown with yellow dentates. Everywhere, from beaches to rocky, alpine areas.

• *Tulipa cretica* Boiss.& Heldr.

Perennial small plant, glabrous, with 2-3 leaves

25cm

10cm

II-V

narrow, lanceolate, corrugated, grey-green. Flowers 1-2 with elliptic tepals, 15-32mm long, white or light pink, with yellow throat and anthers. The 3 outer tepals pinkish, dark pink and green hued. At genista fields and rocky areas.

Orchidaceae:

Himantoglossum robertianum (Loisel.) P. Delforge

Tall plant with long- corrugated basal leaves, 7-35cm, fleshy, shiny. Bracts with leaves, violet and dense inflorescence with 12-60 flowers, greenish-red to greenish-violet, with a water-flag scent. Large, trilobate labellum, with a whitish-pink center, wavy edges, bilobate mid-lobe and falciform side-lobes. At meadows, genista fields and sparse forests.

phrys ariadnae *aulus*

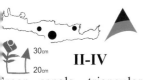

II-IV

ireen sepals, triangular *olourful* petals and *mall*-medium labellum, trilo-*ate*, velvety, black-brown, *ith* close-fitting side-lobes *nd* ovate mid-lobe with *ophisticated* shield, *lue*-grey with a white margin. *mall*, greenish appendix and *potted* cavity without *striction* at shoulder. At *enista* and abandoned fields.

Ophrys basilissa C.& A. Alibertis & Reinhard

I-IV

lant with 2-5 extraordinary *owers*. Green sepals and petals *nd* large labellum, up to 30mm, with a knee-bend at base, dark brown-reddish *elt*, side lobes bending and mid-lobe bending too, with a groove on top. Shield *urrounded* on top by an omega (ω), grey or light blue. The set is similar to *oxing* gloves. At olive groves and genista fields.

Ophrys bombyliflora Link

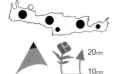

20cm
10cm

II-IV

Small, cute, "teddy-bear", with 2-5 little flowers. Sepals green and petals triangular yellowish-green. Small, ovate, trilobate, brownish-green to dark grey-blue labellum. Extremely hairy side-lobes and round mid-lobe with middle groove. Greyish or violet shield and triangular, folded appendix. At olive groves and abandoned fields.

• *Ophrys fleischmannii* Hayek

Small plant with green petals and sepals. Small-medium labellum, with no groove at

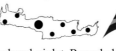

15cm
10cm

II-IV

base, with a knee-bend, velvety, dark red-violet. Rounded side-lobes. Shiny brown or dark blue shield surrounded on top by an omega (ω), whitish. At spars pine-forests, genista fields and olive groves. There's no better velvet!

Ophrys grammica ssp. knossia
(Willing) Alibertis

...all and thin plant with leaves ...hat create a kind of funnel ...round stem. Ovate green ...epals and green-pink petals. Almost square labellum, with small projections ...t base, red-brown, with dark pink small hairs and greenish appendix. H-shaped ...hield, purple-lilac to silvery and green eye-like shapes.

50cm
15cm
I-IV

• *Ophrys mesaritica*
Paulus
& C.& A. Alibertis

XII-III

Similar to O. iricolor, but smaller with softer colours. Small-medium spreading labellum, with a slight bend, brown, with a thin, yellow outline. Greyish shield in black-violet hue. Lower part of labellum dark-red, sometimes with a greenish-white center. At genista fields and rocky areas.

Ophrys spruneri
Nyman

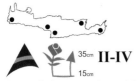

II-IV

One of the most beautiful orchids, whitish to pink-violet sepals, triangular red petals, small-medium labellum, trilobate, black-dark red to brown. Side lobes bending and mid-lobe velvety, folded at edge. H-shaped shield light to dark blue with a light blue outline. Small appendix and blackish eye-like shapes. Between shrubs, abandoned olive groves and genista fields.

Orchis lactea **Poir.**

Robust and beautiful orchid
with 3-8 ovate, lanceolate,
light green leaves and
cylindrical inflorescence with 5-45 scented flowers. Ovate pointy shield, white
o light pink with dark green-grey spots. Small-medium labellum, trilobate, white
o pink-green. Side lobes bending backwards and mid-lobe biolobate, also bend-
ng. Cylindrical, arched button. At genista fields, olive groves and abandoned
ields.

REFERENCES

1.Αλιμπέρτης Αντώνης, **Οι ορχιδέες της Κρήτης και της Καρπάθου**, Ηράκλειο 199?

2.Αλιμπέρης Αντώνης, **Θεραπευτικά, αρωματικά και εδώδιμα φυτά της Κρήτης** Ηράκλειο 2006

3.Αραμπατζής Ι. Θεόδωρος, **Θάμνοι και Δέντρα στην Ελλάδα**, Δράμα 1998

4.Blamey M.& C. Grey Wilson, **Toutes les fleurs de Méditerranée**, Paris 2005

5.Bayer E., Finkenzeller X., Buttler K.P., Grau J., **Guide de la flore méditerranéenne** Paris 1990

6.Boisvert Clotilde, **La cuisine des plantes sauvages**, Paris 1984

7.Γεννάδιος Π, **Λεξικόν Φυτολογικόν**, Αθήνα 1914

8. Γεωργίου Κυριάκος & Δεληπέτρου Πηνελόπη, **Απειλούμενα Ενδημικά Είδη Χλωρίδας στη Νότια Ελλάδα**, Ηράκλειο 2001

9.Delforge Pierre, **Guide des orchidées d'Europe, d'Afrique et du Proche-Orient** Lau-sanne-Paris 1994

10.Διοσκουρίδης, **Περί ύλης ιατρικής**, Αθήνα

11.Fielding John and Turland Nicholas **Flowers of Crete**, Kew 2005

12.Heldreich Χελντραϊχ Θεόδωρος, **Λεξικό των δημωδών ονομάτων των φυτών τη Ελλάδος**, Αθήνα 1980

13.Lipper / Podlech, **Pflanzen der Mittelmeer Küsten**, München 1989

14.Μπάουμαν Έλμουτ, **Η ελληνική χλωρίδα στο μύθο, στην τέχνη και στη λογοτεχνία**, Αθήνα 1984

15.Polunin Oleg, **Flowers of Greece and the Balcans**, Oxford 1987

16.Polunin O. and Huxley A., **Flowers of the Mediterranean**, London 1974

17.Schönfelder Ing. et Pet., **Guide de la Flore Méditerranéenne**, Fribourg 1988

18.Σφήκας Γεώργιος, **Αγριολούλουδα της Κρήτης**, Αθήνα 1987

19.Σφήκας Γεώργιος, **Τα Ενδημικά Φυτά της Ελλάδας**, Αθήνα 1996

20.Strid Arne, **Mountain Flora of Greece**, Cambridge 1986

21.Turland N.J.L. Chitton & J.R. Press, **Flora of the Cretan area**, London 1993

22.Χαβάκης Ιωάννης, **Φυτά και βότανα της Κρήτης**, Αθήνα